You're Smarter Than You Think

Also by Linda Perigo Moore

Does This Mean My Kid's a Genius?

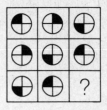

You're Smarter Than You Think

At Least 500 Fun Ways to Expand Your Own Intelligence

LINDA PERIGO MOORE

An Owl Book
Holt, Rinehart and Winston
New York

Library of Congress Cataloging in Publication Data
Moore, Linda Perigo.
You're smarter than you think.
"An Owl book."
Includes bibliographical references and index.
1. Intelligence levels. 2. Genius. 3. Creative
thinking. 4. Intelligence tests. 5. Success. I. Title.
BF431.M622 1984   153   84-6685
ISBN 0-03-063858-5

First Edition

Design by Barbara M. Marks
Printed in the United States of America
10 9 8 7 6 5 4 3 2 1

Grateful acknowledgment is made for permission to quote from the following
works:
Side Effects by Woody Allen. Copyright © 1980. Reprinted by permission of
Random House, Inc. Publishers; *Torrance Tests of Creative Thinking* by E.
Paul Torrance. Copyright © 1962 by Scholastic Testing Service, Inc. Reprinted by permission of Scholastic Testing Service, Inc., from: *The Manual of
the Logical Reasoning Test; Threshold Limit Values* 1983–84 edition. Copyright © 1983 by the American Conference of Governmental Industrial Hygienists, Inc. Reprinted by permission of American Conference of Governmental
Industrial Hygienists, Inc.; *Topology: The Rubber-Sheet Geometry* by Donovan Johnson, et al. Copyright © 1960, Webster Publishing, Inc.; *Effective
Business Writing*, Second Edition, by Linda Comerford, Leslie Kelly, and
Linda Perigo Moore. Copyright © 1982 by Kelly & Associates. Reprinted by
permission of Kelly & Associates; *Plot Titles Test* by Raymond Berger and J.
P. Guilford, Copyright © 1969. Reprinted by permission of Sheridan Psychological Services, Inc. Orange, California; *Flanagan Aptitude Classification
Test, Ingenuity.* Copyright © 1957 by John C. Flanagan, and the *Flanagan Industrial Test, Ingenuity.* Copyright © 1960 by John C. Flanagan. By permission of the publisher, Science Research Associates, Inc.

ISBN 0-03-063858-5

For Stuart

Acknowledgments

Sincere gratitude to Patricia Connor McReynolds, gifted-education consultant, for this project. Her support and generous loan of research materials have been invaluable.

Additional thanks to my family and friends who, perhaps without knowing it, offered encouragement when it truly made a difference.

Thank you to Amy Berkower of Writers House. Amy had confidence in me when this book was merely a couple of loose paragraphs.

However, my deepest gratitude goes to my editor, Judy Karasik. I cursed her name in the night because of the changes she suggested, the jokes she said didn't work, and the way she gently pushed me to do more. But as you read this book, you should know that she made it better.

Contents

Preface

Genius is a novelty. But it shouldn't be. Nothing in biological, educational, or anthropological research proves that any of us was ever intended to think with a radically different physical mechanism. There can be disruptions in the normal pattern of thoughts: destructive events such as disease, trauma, or genetic malfunction can befall anyone. But each healthy human brain *should* be capable of everything possible for *any* human brain. Most of our differences, then, are ones of learning bias, personal motivation, and opportunity of time, place, and degree.

This book will demonstrate:

How your intellectual potential may have gone unrecognized both by society and by yourself.

How you may have achieved superior intelligence despite an inferior school experience.

How you can *still* utilize the best of educational technology to increase your intelligence even more.

How you can remove some of the solemnity from life's greatest adventures: thought and imagination.

What if you really *are* smarter than you think? What if the measurements of childhood (like the IQ score) were wrong? What if you have yet to recognize your accomplishments in adult learning, problem solving, and intellectual growth? What if you have missed the best of educational technology? It's still available. What if you are—in fact—a lost genius?

Take this test and find out.

The "Lost Genius" Self-Evaluation
(Which items are correct or most often correct?)

1. When I was in school, I never studied but I could usually make my way through any test.

2. I know pretty much where everything is located in my house. If one of the kids asks for the stakes to the camping tent, I remember that we stored them in the garage closet, next to the Christmas decorations.

3. I never read the instructions. I can usually figure it out by myself.

4. I never forget a face. If I recognize someone on a TV commercial, I'll rack my brain until I remember where I saw her before.

5. I could always memorize enough to ace a test, but the information would be gone the next day.

6. Whenever I look at an IQ or achievement-test question, I can see why several of the answers could be correct.

7. I couldn't remember dates in history class, but I always understood the general idea of where things were going.

8. I'm good at anticipating the answers to riddles, puzzles, and quiz shows like "Password" and "The $25,000 Pyramid."

9. I can see something funny in almost every situation. It's been embarrassing at times.

10. Sometimes when I'm explaining an idea, other ideas force themselves into my thoughts until it's hard to keep my mind on what I'm talking about.

11. I'm pretty good at puns. When life gets tense at the office, I always have a wisecrack.

12. I have an ear for accents. I can usually tell if a person's from Canada, Virginia, or the Carolinas by the way he pronounces vowels.

13. I can tell if somebody is singing off-key.

14. I'm good at judging distances and sizes.

15. I help my friends balance their checkbooks and/or do their taxes.

16. When I drive the car pool, kids who won't behave have to run alongside of the car.

17. My boss is a fool.

18. If I'm painting the kitchen I remove all food and dishes from the countertops, tape paper over the cabinets, and shake the paint

can before opening it. If the color isn't just right, I do the job over again.

19. I can visualize the path I took and the objects I saw during the last visit I made to a museum.

20. I work the crosswords in ink.

21. My (office desk, personal space, bathroom drawer) is completely organized. Pens, stamps, and paper clips are segregated in the middle drawer. Bottles are arranged according to function and frequency of usage.

22. I eavesdrop on conversations in restaurants.

23. I know the birth dates of all my cousins' children.

24. I can always pick my kids out in a crowd. They're the ones with the red balloons taped to their heads.

25. I have very little tolerance when a staff meeting or public forum drifts into an orgiastic glorification of trivia.

26. The calendar at my desk, in my kitchen, or on my wrist currently shows the correct date.

27. I read vocabulary builders and word-power paperbacks. I try to learn a new word almost every day.

28. My garage, attic, car trunk, and closets are full of things I'll probably use someday.

29. When I enter a bookstore I take time to browse, can read titles on the shelves without tilting my head 90 degrees, and buy more than what I came in for.

30. I watch PBS more often than any other TV channel. (Add a bonus point if you also sent in your subscription.)

31. When I try out a new recipe, I add whatever additional ingredients seem to go with it. I never measure.

32. I was valedictorian of my high school class.

33. I can remember the name of my high school. (Add half a bonus point if you can also remember the full name of your high school principal.)

34. I never go to Avon, real estate, or Tupperware parties. If I want what they're selling, I'll call an order in to the home office.

35. When I'm engaged in conversation, I can completely tune out the other person and he'll never even know it.

36. I can list the seven countries of Central America.

37. I knew there *were* seven countries in Central America. (Subtract three points if you didn't know Mexico was NOT one of the seven. Add ten bonus points if you know whether Central America is topographically a part of the South or North American continent.)

38. I save *National Geographics* and store them in chronological order.

39. I know Shakespeare's real intent when he wrote, "To thine own self be true." (Add two bonus points if you also know the character that said it.)

40. Wherever I work, I write my own job description.

41. I can sketch a human face and the nose looks like a real nose.

42. I know the answer to the following: If it takes Big Ben thirty seconds to strike six o'clock, how long does it take to strike midnight?

43. I do filing, use the dictionary, or find a number in the phone book without having to sing the alphabet song.

44. I know who invented the automobile. (I'll give you a hint: it wasn't Henry Ford.)

45. I can subtotal my groceries, right along with the cashier.

46. I can name all of the Smurfs, Santa's reindeer, the seven Dwarfs, or the starting defensive team for the Dallas Cowboys. (There are indeed eleven rather than seven Cowboys, but anyone who chooses this option won't mind.)

47. When some fool has swiped the unit pricing stickers from the grocery shelf, I can still tell if king size on sale is cheaper than family size with a coupon.

48. I know that Kafka is not an ethnic bread.

49. I really do understand how a computer functions—honest.

Scoring

Score 2 points for each item checked.

90–100	Congratulations. You're a possible genius.
50–89	Lots of hope here. Definitely gifted caliber.
10–49	Maybe, if you study each chapter.
1–9	Forget it. You need a different book.

Bonus Section

ADD 2 points for every magazine subscription you read regularly. *TV Guide* or the *Horchow Catalog* don't count.
ADD 10 points for each additional test item you thought of.
ADD 90 points to your total if you challenged the scoring and
   discovered the one test item NOT representing genius potential.

(P.S.: It does not take Big Ben sixty seconds to strike midnight. See chapter 5 to find out why.)

You're Smarter
Than You Think

Genius and Other Oddities: The Gifted Adult

You could be much smarter than you think. It's even possible that you could be a genius. This is because:

- Genius is the synonym for ultimate intelligence.
- Given appropriate opportunity and instruction, any healthy, adequately motivated individual can learn intelligence.
- Therefore, any healthy, adequately motivated individual can ultimately learn to be a genius.

All evidence for such a conclusion comes from educational research and practice with gifted children, for it's within this group of accelerated learners that educators have identified those individuals well along the path to levels of accomplishment the rest of us call genius.

Superior educational methods developed for gifted children can help you to think better as an adult. Moreover, those intellectual traits that educators and psychologists have identified in these children can help you discover your own adult gifted ability and genius potential. The gift, then, is there for the taking.

My conviction that what works for gifted kids can work for

adults began in October 1981. At that time I was publicizing a book about gifted children. By exposing the educational and behavioral problems of this group I had expected two diverse reactions: (1) recognition by parents that their little Jason, Mandy, or Amy Lou was, indeed, a gifted child; and, (2) blatant hostility toward the suggestion those students with the greatest displays of talent, intellect, and creativity may in some way be educationally handicapped. *Many* parents did bring forth previously unidentified gifted children, but in place of hostility, I heard pleading for more gifted education in the public and private school systems. I heard from parents who had been told their children were "too smart," or "reading beyond their levels" or "overachieving." I heard of children crying at the start of dreary, boring school days. I heard from a high school valedictorian who hated school so much that she waxed apples at an orchard rather than go to college. Most parents were starved for the information necessary to identify, nurture, and challenge a gifted child. (Naturally, I suggested they tuck my book under the kid's pillow.)

But then I was astonished by a third and unexpected response. It would usually begin like this: "I don't have children but what you've been describing is just what happened to me when I was in school."

During every interview and at every speech I would define those behavioral characteristics that illustrate gifted children. "These are kids who can memorize an entire episode of 'Gilligan's Island,'" I would say. "They rip open Christmas toys to see how they work; they quit the soccer team if they can't be the forward; they slam the Atari across the room when they don't win; they often fail, give up, or snub their noses at the school system; they display an early and advanced use of the language; they are aggressive, challenging, and intolerant. Worse than that, they are most often annoyingly correct."

Soon I realized that if I were conducting a thirty-minute radio phone-in interview, four of the seven callers would not be asking about their gifted children. They would be asking about themselves.

A man from Seattle phoned the "America Overnight" program: "I had a terrible time concentrating on my schoolwork. I was always being yelled at for daydreaming. I flunked out of two universities before I settled down. Now I'm an aerospace engineer."

After a speech in Chicago, a gray-haired woman approached me, "I always thought there was something wrong with me and the way I looked at things. I never dreamed I was gifted."

One listener phoned a Baltimore station, "I have a thirty-year-old son who was a gifted child. I'm fifty-five and I was a gifted child. My eighty-year-old mother was a gifted child. And the schools ruined us all."

Let's get this point straight: As long as there have been children, there have been gifted children. Plato discussed accelerated learners, as did the ancient Chinese. In this country some of the most significant research and opinion regarding the gifted education of potential geniuses was produced in the 1930s by a superior educator, Leta Hollingworth.[1] Her work was preceded several decades before in Italy by Dr. Maria Montessori.[2]

I had been addressing the problems of today's children, but children with accelerated intellectual development, unusual talents, and highly creative minds have always been around. They did not suddenly spring forth like the mold on last week's leftovers. What about the gifted children who attended school ten, twenty, or thirty years ago? Surely some have become scientists, statesmen, scholars, and rodeo stars—but what has happened to all of "last season's gifts"?

I came to recognize a great many adults who:

- felt their intellectual and creative abilities were never advanced by their school experiences;
- wondered if the new approaches to educating the gifted would have made a difference for them;
- with appropriate education, might have developed levels of genius;
- may have already taught themselves to be more intelligent than they realize.

IN THE FIRST PLACE— WHAT'S INTELLIGENCE?

Your intelligence is defined from two perspectives: your own and that shared by others.

Your Own Definition

In the privacy of your thoughts, do you describe yourself as being very smart? This intellectual self-image evolves from millions of minuscule encounters with other people. Did you ever score higher than the smartest kid in the class? Did your parents tell you that you could do anything you set your mind to? Did your classmates call you stupid? Did a teacher laugh at something you took seriously? Did you believe "them" or did you turn around (even if only in your mind) and tell them they were wrong? Take a look at your basic assumptions—the ones you've had since childhood. They contain the reasons why you may not think of yourself as being genius material.

- *Your beliefs about your intelligence quotient.*
  Is your IQ *high enough?* Do you believe you have the physical ability (mental capacity) to be a genius?
- *School—either your personal progress or the overall quality of the system.*
  Were you smart in school? Was your *school* smart (academically advanced)? Are you too academically retarded to catch up with the geniuses? Is it just too big a task for you now?
- *Your biases about how intelligence relates to such diverse subjects as emotional stability and aging.*
  Are geniuses really sort of crazy? Is it emotionally safer to be intellectually average?
  Is it generally true that old people are not as smart as they were when they were young? How much intelligence do they actually lose?

Let's look at each of these areas and try to determine whether or not you should believe genius is possible for you.

The Big IQ

Many adults still interpret intelligence with the most prominent measurement of childhood. If you really *had* to, you could quote that junior high IQ score, couldn't you? But despite layers of societal reverence and myth, the IQ test is, and always has been, just a proficiency gauge of a few simple steps in childlike thinking patterns. We will examine this fact in great detail in chapter 2, but for now, think back to your adolescence. When you were insulted, when your feelings were hurt, when you were scolded for misbehavior—how did you react? Did you sometimes cry? The fact that you cried *then* does not necessarily mean that now as an adult you cry when the boss gives you a reprimand. In this same way, your junior high IQ score is not necessarily representative of your current intelligence, thinking patterns, and potentials. Maybe you've grown up—and maybe you have not.

School Daze

Success in school is another measurement of childhood accomplishment often misapplied to adult intelligence. Such success can either be your own, or the proficiency of the school system itself. I made high marks in school. I benefited from that accomplishment and I thoroughly enjoyed those benefits. Now I'm a parent and an educator. I want my child to enjoy all the good things that can come to him because of a solid academic foundation. But it would be irrational for me to believe that success in school automatically correlates with adult intelligence or accomplishment. This is because intelligence is not mere scorekeeping. It's not even the acquisition of specific bits of information. It is instead a personal assimilation of a specific educational technology. Intelligence is learning *how* to learn and then transferring that skill to real-life problem solving.

If you were fortunate enough to have had a skillful teacher, you probably learned more, regardless of your grades, than did someone with a less skillful teacher. The elements of this technology can advance the learning skills, accomplishment levels, and thus intelligence of most who are willing to put them into practice.

In the past, few children received what we now recognize as a gifted education. Many school systems simply had neither the resources nor the inclination to meet the special needs of accelerated learners. Your chances of being identified as a gifted child were best if you either stood out like a whale in a swimming pool, or if you behaved just like a miniature teacher.[3]

In addition, parents and educators of accelerated learners have demonstrated that even when identified, it can be the *most* intelligent or *most* creative child who fails in school. This usually occurs when the gifted child cannot sustain interest in a system that presents no intellectual challenge.

When he was a student at the Royal College, Louis Pasteur's teachers listed his progress and academic standing in chemistry as *mediocre*. One of Beethoven's first music teachers is remembered only by the often quoted evaluation, "As a composer, he is hopeless." The principle extends to adults in the workplace. F. W. Woolworth was not allowed to wait on customers when employed in a dry-goods store because his supervisor felt he "didn't have enough sense." And some long-forgotten newspaper editor fired Walt Disney because, as his employment file reads: "He had no good ideas."[4]

Evaluating Your Own Prior Access to Gifted Education

By now your memory banks should be retrieving rather specific associations between potential genius (gifted) behavior and your own past educational opportunities. Maybe you received instruction that was intended to encourage your potential. Maybe you didn't.[5]

Educational research has recently focused upon the kinds of learning environments and instructional techniques most effective with accelerated learners. Dr. Emily Stewart surveyed six hundred students and found that those previously identified as gifted preferred classes emphasizing independent study, discussion, and analysis. Other students preferred instructional settings with more structure, such as lectures and specifically defined projects.[6] Which teaching method typified your own school days? Was it appropriate to your needs?

Perhaps you struggled through dull, unimaginative schoolwork. Churchill called his classroom experiences the "long, gray days." (He also flunked the sixth grade.[7]) Perhaps you were the creative child whose creativity was squelched in a system of education that allowed only one correct answer for each question. Perhaps you were gifted in a specific discipline not covered in the school curriculum. Then, perhaps, you would have known the answers to different questions. At one point in your school career you may have been unable to endure another dismal, uninspiring, unchallenging lesson plan. Perhaps as a result you chose *not* to parrot Euclidean geometry back to the teacher; or perhaps you decided Nathaniel Hawthorne was a raging bore, unworthy of your time and energy. Perhaps you decided—much too prematurely—to think for yourself.

But perhaps you *never* thought of yourself as being "gifted."

Perhaps you should have.

"Ol' Weird Harold"

The most tragic and irrational impediment to the achievement of ultimate knowledge is the way we have been taught to *fear* genius. You may even have private fears that there is real danger in being "too smart."

"There is no great genius without some touch of madness."
—Seneca, 4 B.C.–65 A.D.

And according to Seneca, Plato and Aristotle felt the same.

The image of progressing up an intellectual incline, reaching genius, and then dropping off into an abyss of madness and insanity has endured as a foreboding adage. The idea was nurtured in our recent psyche by none other than Sigmund Freud. Poor ol' Freud. The things people now say about him would have broken his mother's heart. Nevertheless, he did perpet-

uate—both in theory and through a cadre of fervent disciples—
the notion that you could be too smart for your own good. Many
of his essays dealt with the suggestion that psychopathology is
a common finding in the life of a *true genius*.

A 1980 issue of the *American Journal of Psychoanalysis*
cites Shakespeare, Einstein, Michelangelo, and Freud himself
as having "a history of restraint, discipline and organization
forcing them into a state of split ego and ambivalence. Resultant creativity and genius," the article continues ". . . were reactions to and a way of dealing with [this state]."[8]

Weird persons of high intelligence have always been the
ultimate bogeymen. Somehow the crazed killer smart enough
to outfox you or catch you off guard is more chilling than the
run-of-the-mill crazed killer. As an adolescent I was terrified
by the fictional genius who was so clever that he dissolved his
victims in a bathtub full of acid and then washed them down the
drain. Because of the crazed and cunning character created by
Anthony Perkins and Alfred Hitchcock, I still cannot take a
shower without first bolting the bathroom door. (Only reason
and strong will have maintained my personal hygiene over the
years.)

Science fiction movies of the 1950s and 1960s usually por-
trayed alien intelligence as superior intelligence intent upon
dominating us, physically occupying us or sapping our minds of
vital normalcy. Even on "Star Trek," no occupied human ever
liked the benefits of having a superior alien brain.

And yet for every maniac genius making the movies and
front pages—ten thousand socially adaptable and generally
banal ones go unmentioned. Everyone must leap emotional
hurdles in order to grow and mature, and the intellectually advanced individual is no different.[9] But with regard to serious
social conflict, countless researchers have cited lower delinquency rates among gifted adolescents and young adults,[10] as
well as lower recidivism among those who do commit crimes.[11]
When sociologists and psychologists have probed the motiva-
tions of genius criminals, they have found that most of these individuals—just like most other criminals—have come from

environments of child abuse, degradation, anger, and hostility.[12] Social deviance, then, is far more complicated than simply being smart.

Old Dogs and New Tricks

Your intellectual self-image is also influenced by your beliefs about aging and learning. There is a general perception, often bolstered by psychological research, that:

- aging means you can't learn as easily as before;
- aging means that you forget what you learned earlier.

But such conclusions about aging and intelligence are shallow. While conditions such as senile dementia and Alzheimer's disease epitomize the inevitability of aging and cognitive loss, researchers at Johns Hopkins University estimate that less than 5 percent of the general population ever suffer such severe mental dysfunction. And only an additional 10 percent of aged individuals exhibit other types of mild to moderate abnormalities in cognition.[13]

The most current educational research now verifies that, for the rest of us, learning skills *do not* diminish with old age. Speed of recall diminishes with old age. When they are given enough time, healthy eighty-year-olds score just as well on intelligence tests as do healthy twenty-year-olds.

So why did earlier research projects record general declines in intelligence test scores as individuals grow older? The answer comes in a startling conclusion from a research team at Texas Technological University. Reviewing hundreds of these past studies, the researchers observed that the expected declines had not occurred when aged subjects were free from neurological disease, or had registered either high IQ scores or higher education levels at earlier ages.[14] But the most significant observation of both the Texas team and of other researchers (such as Alexander Reeves, chairman of the Dartmouth Medical School's department of neurology)[15] was that research data is usually gathered in clinical settings where test participants are subject to neurological disease and subject to clinical depression because of living patterns.

Few researchers interrupt a corporate executive or a jogging senior citizen with, "Would you mind completing this IQ test?" They go instead to institutions of the discarded, displaced, and ill.

Similar conclusions are coming in from all over the world:

- A Scandinavian psychologist conducted a five-year longitudinal study of 768 subjects, aged seventy to seventy-five. The only significant declines in the intelligence and memory occurred among those subjects with cardiovascular disease.[16]
- In Germany, in 1980, two studies concluded that rather than a decline in intelligence, seventy-year-old subjects displayed declines in the ability to adapt to those changes in social environments that resulted in poor nutrition, poor living standards, and depression.[17]
- A British researcher reconfirmed previous studies that verbal and nonverbal divergent thinking (creativity) differs from traditional IQ and that this difference becomes greater both with age and with aging females.[18] Translation: Everyone gets more creative with age—and women even more so.
- Three separate reports to the *Journal of Experimental Child Psychology* concluded that adults are more efficient than children when retrieving long-term stored data. Long-term memory consists of putting items into associate groupings, and adults do this better.[19]
- Women, ages twenty to seventy, were tested on perceptual problem-solving strategies (the visual problems seen on IQ tests: folding paper boxes, rotating sticks, etc.). Results indicated that while older subjects needed more time to solve the problems, this was caused by decreased eyesight rather than higher-order cognitive-process decline.[20] (Let's hear it for more ophthalmic research.)

• Dr. Muriel Oberledger, a California psychologist, writes that older individuals display memory loss because they:

> have more to remember;
> choose to ignore or discount details in preference to abstract conclusions;
> have learned to expect memory loss;
> often lose the motivation to remember because of depression over aging and anxiety caused by illness and physical incapacities.

Dr. Oberledger concludes that older adults remember what they are "interested in remembering."[21]

Finally, although adults think and learn in ways different from children, they are usually observed with reference to models of youthful intelligence.

Gerontologist Gisela Labouvie-Vief contends that our assumptions about the patterns of intellectual development and maturation stop short at adulthood.[22] Certainly for many educators and educational systems the primary perception of adulthood is as an ending to childhood. This is because human-development concepts have come from child-centered theorists such as Swiss zoologist Jean Piaget. It was Piaget who (after studying other animals) developed the concept that human beings progress through a series of developmental growth stages that are usually, but not always, linked to chronological age. He believed that the final stage of intellectual growth took place near physical adolescence when most individuals finally learned to differentiate between the real and the possible. He called this state of deductive certainty *logical positivism* and concluded that all subsequent learning merely stabilized and reinforced that which the subject had already come to believe.[23]

Thus Labouvie-Vief believes that educators and psychologists have never given full recognition to the environmental constraints upon adult learning, nor have they fully accounted for the conflicts between feelings and intellect which are so prevalent in adult decision making.[24] Translation: learning for adults is more susceptible to distractions and decisions *not* to learn than is learning for children. (God knows you'd love to re-read Melville or bone up on those Econ. 101 theories, but the teapot's whistling, the roof's leaking, and baby needs shoes.)

Labouvie-Vief suggests that adults progress through two additional developmental stages. In the first, logical absolut-ism ("I don't care what you say, by God, I know I'm right!") comes in conflict with logical relativism ("Well, actually, it doesn't seem to work that way in real life."). For many, this stage can last from adolescence into middle age. Young adults, for example, usually focus upon logical and semantic *surface* re-lationships of a problem. These bits of reasoning are often iso-lated and abstract. There is a primary search for the always correct or ideal solution and a disillusionment when life de-viates from theory.

The second stage of adulthood occurs when you become more reliant upon yourself when making decisions. You make firm decisions about personal values, ethics, goals, and convic-tions. You finally feel *grown up*. The mature adult, then, eval-uates elements of a problem not only with regard to logic and correctness, but also with regard to other matrices such as so-cial well-being, the good of the community, goals for the family, and personal needs and goals.

Many other researchers have confirmed this concept. Older adults are more likely to use an interdependence of in-tellectual functions when solving a problem than are younger adults.[25] A clinical observer could label this kind of thinking as *illogical*, and thus conclude that older individuals decline in logical functioning. But an equally valid conclusion is that such a pattern reflects a skill called *compromise*. Unfortunately, compromise—a creative resolution to the constraints of real-ism—doesn't show up on anybody's test of genius.

And so, the way *you* assess your own intelligence is a com-posite of several factors: old measurements of childhood, how you fared in the school system, and the experiences, beliefs, and biases making up your intellectual self-image. But others define your intelligence in other ways.

It's Not Genius Until They *Say It's Genius*

There's a practical credo about insanity that you are insane when people stand off in a corner, look at you, and say to one another: "You know—that guy's really crazy!" Intelligence is a lot like that, too.

With no intended insult to poets, philosophers, cabbages, and kings, the *professional* or *working* definitions of intelligence have evolved from two distinctly different vantage points: psychology and education.

While no single psychologist is like every other psychologist and no single teacher is like every other teacher, the two tribes sprang from distinctly opposite attitudes regarding the origins of intelligence. This dichotomy is embodied as the classic nature/nurture debate. Whether expressed as: "Good ol' Mom and Dad—thank God and/or the chemistry of the stars— they gave me enough!" *or* "Damn their sheepskins for stopping my piano lessons," all educational and psychological theories of intelligence exist within the context of origin.

Psychologists have devised an elaborate, often overwhelmingly impressive mathematical scale by which to edify prominent psychological theories of the nature and origins of intelligence. And while individual psychologists have significantly advanced the concept of learned intelligence, the basis of all intellectual testing—both IQ and aptitude—is the unmistakable assumption that every human being has a *specifically measurable amount* of intellectual capacity.

We could call this the Psychological Pot Theory. I've got a pot, you've got a pot. My pot's different from yours because I had different ancestors and different prenatal nutrition. If my pot's twice as big as yours, I could fill mine half full; you could fill yours to the rim and we would still be of equal intelligence. But if I would add a little bit more, you'd be out of luck because then I'd be smarter, and smarter forever. In this hereditary container theory of intelligence, the achievement test is the dipstick of accomplishment; an IQ or aptitude is the size of your vessel, and *genius* is a pretty big one. The greatest support for this way of looking at intelligence comes from members of high-IQ clubs.

Educators look upon the acquisition of intelligence as a task to be completed. Theirs is the role of a practitioner: herding sweating little bodies on dusty playgrounds; picking the path through fact and fantasy; and patiently guiding intellectual evolution with a bold, red grading pencil. The very structure of this role gives them little opportunity for reflection upon theoretical origins or influences of intelligence. Most educators care less about "How Johnny got to be so smart" and more about "What can I do to keep Johnny challenged today?" For this reason educational definitions of intelligence usually consist not of test scores but of behavioral characteristics describing the task in progress.

The dichotomy between these two disciplines became most apparent when the psychological theories of how intelligence should develop conflicted with the educational observations of how intelligence functions. This is because the psychologists' tests of intelligence did not cover all of the intellectual functioning observed by the educators. And there is a distinct difference between potential as a pot to be filled and potential as a pot to be constructed.

How Accelerated Learning, High Intelligence, and Genius All Became Such a Gift

Many people think "gifted" is a modern label, but Francis Galton coined the word in an 1869 psychological report entitled, "Hereditary Genius: An Inquiry into Its Laws and Consequences."[26] At this juncture, scholars from both education and psychology turned from the earlier notions of genius as adult accomplishment and began to focus upon the predictability of genius through the observations of the child prodigy. Giftedness came to mean *potential genius*. It's important to note that for almost one hundred years, most subsequent educators and psychologists defined giftedness as purely academic display. Factors such as creativity, artistic display, and human-relations skills were considered irrelevant to the concept.

Hundreds of psychological and educational theories and

speculations of giftedness flourished until the next milestone: Lewis Terman's 1925 longitudinal studies, *Genetic Studies of Genius: Mental and Physical Traits of Gifted Children.*[27] The Terman study was the first to follow a large group of gifted children as they progressed from potential to adulthood. His observations forever cemented the concept of predictability because *most* of his subjects fulfilled what he felt was a divine prophecy and became highly productive, successful—sometimes even genius—adults.

Calling potential genius "the gift"—something bestowed from an omnipotent benefactor—was no accident. Galton, Terman, and countless psychologists of both eras believed completely in the hereditary nature of intelligence. Whether calling the benefactor divine or Darwinian, they believed you either had the gift or you did not. The IQ test (originally intended for the educational placement of mentally retarded children) was applied to all children in an attempt to spot genius at an early age and thus give it proper educational focus. And at least "giving educational focus" was an idea upon which the psychologists and the educators could agree.

A few dissenters regularly challenged the opinions concerning hereditary intelligence, publishing articles declaring that genius could and should be taught to great numbers of children. But their words had little impact upon educational practice. Psychologists laid out the parameters for identifying and verifying just which children had genius potential, while educators passed out standardized test papers, gathered results, and dutifully recorded IQ scores in student records. Educators rarely implemented plans designed to truly challenge gifted children, let alone techniques that would bring ignored potential to light. The focus on giftedness waned. But once the process was set in motion, IQ scores continued to accumulate.

Then in 1957 the story took a radical twist. Russia's German scientists (as opposed to our German scientists) beat us into space. That's when hereditary genius began to falter. The public turned to the educators and cried, "What the hell's going on here?" The educators turned to the psychologists and cried, "What the hell's going on here? Surely the Germans don't have that many genetically superior minds. We won the war; Hitler was a madman! They must have *taught* Sputnik into orbit!" The pathways of traditional education and psychology separated a bit farther.

It was still a relatively esoteric debate until 1971 when U.S. Commissioner of Education Sidney P. Marland prompted Congress to create the Office of Gifted and Talented. This action caused educators to reexamine the use of IQ tests as the principal means of identifying potential genius. The IQ is a simple measurement of six to eight specific mental processes, while observations of functioning intelligence have yielded as many as 120 thinking processes. Skills such as creativity and complex problem solving were in no way addressed by the old psychological intelligence tests. Therefore giftedness in its more expansive definition came to be the portal for all those learned, bright, gregarious, creative, and talented students who blocked on IQ tests.

Calling potential genius "the gift" is truly a misnomer, for it is not something that is granted to or found in but a few. Giftedness is an accelerated step on the path to genius. More important, it is a step you may have reached without even knowing it.

Spotting What Others Would Call Your Gift

Since you may not have the scarlet "G" in plain sight, the factors with which educators now identify gifted students can help you evaluate your own adult levels of intellectual functioning. This identification process began with the Marland report, but hundreds of gifted educators have contributed to a general examination of how accelerated learners think and solve problems.

Two major scales have emerged in these efforts.

U.S. Office of Education Guidelines

During the mid-1970s, while director of the Office of Gifted and Talented, Dr. Dorothy Sisk prepared with her staff a list of behavioral characteristics observed in children believed to be accelerated learners. (These observations were both their own and those reported in educational literature.) The list was distributed by the U.S. Office of Education and has subsequently been used as a keynote for most other attempts to identify gifted students.

As you read the following, keep in mind that the classification was always intended to be a generalization. A person rarely exhibits high levels of all traits at all times. The characteristics are:

Early and advanced use of vocabulary
Keen observation and curiosity
Retention of a variety of information
Periods of intense concentration
Ability to understand complex concepts, perceive relationships, and think abstractly
A broad and changing spectrum of interests
Strong critical thinking skills and self-criticism
Early demonstration of talents in music, art, athletics, and/or the performing arts[28]

When applied to adult behavior the list can take on a new perspective.

Early and Advanced Use of Vocabulary   The two major components of language sophistication are both speech and reading levels accelerated beyond chronological peers. Many children later identified as being gifted have also been described as "self-taught" readers. This phenomenon appears to be a subtle blending of a good memory, strong abstract reasoning skills, opportunity, modeling (somebody reading to them), and positive reinforcement.

"Marge!! Did you hear this? My God, Junior's reading! Come on, honey, say it again for Daddy—*dog*. There! He did it again!"

Regardless of how the skill is acquired, gifted children usually enjoy reading and whip through any book several grade levels ahead of the pack. A first grader reading on a fifth-grade level, or a two-year-old reading the newspaper—neither would be extraordinary in the annals of giftedness. Yet be aware of significant exceptions before phoning your relatives and asking

precisely when you began to speak and read. Einstein didn't ut-
ter a comprehensible word until he was four. That qualifies for
a label of "educable retarded" on several scales of intellectual
development. And the life of Helen Keller should remind us all
of the special problems for the gifted individual who also happens to have severe communication disorders.

Because of the structured and time-honored correlation
between vocabulary and intelligence, the *advanced* portion of
the formula is more significant to adults. In his book *Intelligence Can Be Taught*, psychologist Arthur Whimbey explains
the correlation this way: "Vocabulary knowledge is an end
product of . . . the skill of comprehension. In other words, vocabulary knowledge accumulates and is practiced in the course
of fully comprehending verbal ideas, and as such, it is a good
indicator of overall intelligence."[29]

All of this is to say that if you have a penchant for vocabulary, whiz through the crosswords, regularly peruse the thesaurus, can decipher anagrams at a glance, and understand
absolutely everything William F. Buckley utters—you're a
gifted adult. But note an additional point. If, when you do not
understand Buckley, you rush to the dictionary, comprehend,
remember, and subsequently work some obscure eighteenth-
century slogan into your next chat with the baby-sitter—then,
by every accepted definition of giftedness, you are also a gifted
adult.

Keen Observation and Curiosity   Everybody knows
Tonto's horse was a pinto named Scout. But a gifted adult
might remember the placement of that horse's brown
splotches. A curious gifted adult might take a moment to
thumb through a pictorial essay of 1950s TV stars just to check
it out. Did that large spot surround the left or the right portion
of Scout's face? (By the way, what is the correct term for a
horse's face, anyway?)

Some gifted adults can look at an individual for sixty seconds, turn away, and describe every article of clothing, jew-
elry, and assorted appurtenances—complete with label
identification, probable price, and place of purchase.

The keenest observers generally turn out to be professional or amateur artists. That's why teaching a child to sketch—to observe and reinforce detail through a secondary sense—endures as a hallmark of intellectual instruction. (Ever try drawing a duck when you've never bothered to really look at one? Oh, sure, you can pick it out in a crowd—but that's not the same.)

Even as adults, individuals with high levels of observation and curiosity tend to be experiential learners. Preferring to rip open the box without reading the instructions, they also investigate noises in the night, seize opportunities to eavesdrop, and forever ask "Why" and "How do you know?"

Retention of a Variety of Information   Have you ever played bridge with one of those annoying people who can remember every card trumped, every bid made, and every mathematical combination within the realm of slam probability? After bidding, before the dummy can lay down a card, this character will say: "We'll give you two diamond tricks and the rest are ours." I hate that. But it is an example of the kind of memory factored into the definition of giftedness. Research into the intellectual functioning of chess masters, for example, has revealed that these individuals generally memorize patterns of standardized attack and defense strategies. When given memory tests utilizing other factors, they exhibit recall no better or worse than other subjects who have not been trained.[30]

So, memory relies in great measure upon the degree of subject commitment—how much you *want* to remember. "Do you remember that party in the eighth grade when you and Cheryl Barnes showed up in identical dresses?" I am continually astounded at my mother's ability to recall the most insignificant details of my youth. I don't even remember Cheryl Barnes—let alone a party dress. The ability to recall large quantities of data about a specific subject and minute details of an obscure one represent a vital component of giftedness. Many college professors earn their livelihoods and many gifted adults amuse their friends with astonishing presentations of trivia.

When you were a kid this skill could have earned you many

bonus points as an *ideal student*—every teacher's dream. Your ability to memorize would have been invaluable when recalling and repeating just what the teacher wanted to hear. But had you been interested in an atypical or noncurricular subject— something like medieval heraldry, Indian mythology, or the epistemological strategies and cultural ramifications of Donkey Kong—well, tough luck.

Periods of Intense Concentration   It could be called the Thomas Edison School of Perspiratory Genius. Biographers report that Edwin Land, of Polaroid fame, spends weeks at a time concentrating upon specific details of an elusive problem. He literally bolts the laboratory door and sends out for sandwiches.

Many educational theorists believe this facility to spend enough time in concerted mental effort and focus is what separates a good idea from the practical application of genius. "Da Vinci may have designed a helicopter," they would say. "But it took another kind of genius to make the thing fly!"

And it certainly didn't escape the feminists of the 1970s that behind every great man *or* woman, there stands a *wife*. Wife being defined as that *someone* who cooks the meals, changes the sheets, and runs the kids to ball practice; someone who performs life's little mundane duties while genius germinates.

But Dr. Sisk was also talking about short periods of intense concentration—particularly in subjects or tasks of one's own choosing.

The "Type A" personality, described by physicians as that high achiever sprinting the path to a breakdown, displays another classic example of gifted behavior. Parents of gifted children often report kids who scream through their days—foot to floorboard—and who must then be forcibly detained at a late-night bedtime. The adult Type-A personalities also display incredibly high energy levels and seem to require very few hours of sleep. Like frantic worker bees, they spend their lives as if personally responsible for the world's entire pollen accumulation.

A gifted child *can* do her homework in front of the TV or

read a book during a tornado alert. A gifted adult can miss the freight train charging through the family room if his team is first-and-goal-to-go. A gifted adult can let the lasagne burn until Renko and Bobby get off the Hill.

My friend Suzanne vacuums carpets with this kind of intensity. One afternoon as she toiled, back bent, face to the floor, her husband entered the house unobserved. The appliance and her eyes met his feet at the same moment. Concentration interrupted, her scream woke the dead and her swing put his leg in a cast.

Ability to Understand Complex Concepts, Perceive Relationships, and Think Abstractly   There are indeed people on the face of this planet who understand the Rubik's cube, who can construct a swing set out of a carton of bolts and rods boxed by some sadist on Taiwan, and who can remember that the nephew of your grandmother is your second cousin once removed. (Or is it the first cousin of your uncle?)

Many gifted individuals are global thinkers. They can't talk about specific trees until they've walked around the forest. Life for them is a series of associations, syntheses, and applications of past events to new situations. B cannot be glued to A until they know the series includes C and D as well. These are the folks who don't get lost the first time they hit St. Louis or the Grand Tetons. They can order and assimilate a thousand little details into a total pattern. They always know where the sun will come up. If they were lucky enough to have been in the Scouts, they got lots of reinforcement for such skills.

Every PTA, hospital board, city council, or neighborhood committee *must* have a concept person who can step back from the discussion and say, "Wait a minute. That won't work. You've got everybody bringing pretzels and beer, and nobody bringing the ice!"

A Broad and Changing Spectrum of Interests   Gifted people collect things. Perhaps such a trait is also connected to the need to make connections and develop relationships: this little piece of junk may someday fit into that little whatever. Words like *pack rat* come to mind.

They also collect experiences. Every time you see this guy

he's off on a new adventure; deeply committed to a different
hobby or indignity; wearing, eating, or relaxing with the latest
fad; or changing careers. Put as gently as possible, many gifted
adults are task hoppers. Their personal and professional ré-
sumés are a string of brief encounters—very often successful,
meaningful, and responsible—but brief, nonetheless. Whether
it's because they lose interest after a success or because they
bolt at conflict—gifted adults are apt to move on.

Strong Critical Thinking Skills and Self-Criticism
Gifted individuals rarely believe something just because you
told them so. They analyze the pros and cons of an issue and
form their own conclusions.

As a student, such behavior can lead to trouble when the
teacher only wants you to regurgitate the facts, opinions, and
conclusions he learned from his own teachers. And it can lead
to disaster on the job when the boss's interpretation of "staying
the course" only means staying *her* course.

The most productive outlets for this trait may include careers in management consulting, literary and artistic criticism,
coaching and education, or any other self-directed, episodic endeavor (like homemaking!).

Self-criticism is in the definition because the gifted are as
demanding of themselves as they are of others. Intrinsic motivation is always touted as a positive educational goal. Being a
self-starter wins points on job evaluations, despite the fact that
no supervisor wants you to start without him. But the extremely motivated individual can establish personal goals that
leave absolutely no room for error. These self-inflicted pres-
sures can permeate all personal, social, and professional relationships, bringing to life the adage that "a genius makes a
terrible employee and an even worse boss."

Gifted educators believe that because of this pressure to
succeed, the gifted individual rarely learns to accept failure.
She will, in fact, avoid competitive situations when victory cannot be assured. Lots of gifted adults won't play racquetball
with you unless you let them win. And if you don't let them win,
they blame their failure on externals: a passing spectator, a

faulty racquet, a dead ball, the court was tilted, etc. We have institutionalized such behavior; it's called the winning spirit.

Others make a mockery of accepted scales of success so they can avoid the possibility of failure. I remember a friend who was always suggesting ideas for novel gadgets and inventions. He discussed the benefits of an inflatable sail and the advantages of a hot-air popcorn popper years before either hit the marketplace. When pressed about developing some of his ideas, he replied, "Are you kidding? That's such a sham. The big corporations just steal it from you anyway."

Educator and psychologist E. Paul Torrance has commented, "Some gifted students consistently fail because they never find anything worthy of their best efforts."[31] Obviously, the same holds true for adults.

Another emotional pitfall for many gifted individuals is the inability to accept supervision or constructive criticism. Every teacher has met a gifted student who cannot—under any circumstances—accept authority. He counterpoints each and every statement, must always have the last word, and is the first to identify mistakes and inconsistencies. Such behavior can interfere with learning. Some teachers respond with subterfuge: "Thank you, Jeffrey. Now will you take these forms to the principal's office?" Some respond with the subconscious resolution to "screw that little buzzard to the space behind the door!"

Gifted adults exhibiting this trait will have a difficult adjustment to group decision making. Forget committee work unless she's in charge. And God save you if you ever have to give one of them an employee evaluation. "What the hell do you mean, I have an antagonistic attitude!"

It is in these areas of easing tensions, tolerating imperfection in themselves and others, and coping with the nongenius aspects of life that many gifted individuals find their greatest challenge.

No man is an island, but for the gifted, it often seems a seductive prospect. In gifted classrooms, one method of handling this phenomenon has been the construction of a classroom space (be it an isolated corner or a pup tent) where the gifted child can elect to simply sit alone and think. It's not uncommon to observe gifted children (even the most gregarious) spending several hours each day in totally self-directed, solitary work or play.

Gifted adults regularly establish such mental and physical periods of escape: working alone on a hobby, shutting out external stimuli with a fine trashy novel, or daydreaming.

Early Demonstration of Talents in Music, Art, and/or the Performing Arts   Obviously Lena Horne and Claude Monet spring to mind, but the definition also includes those people who participate in the Community Thespians' rendition of *Oedipus Rex*, who carry the church choir, and who freehand acrylic quails on the sides of mailboxes.

This category includes those physical skills demonstrated by the gifted athlete. However, most educators recognize that gifted athletes are recipients of the most comprehensive system of gifted education this country provides any of its children. They are:

> identified early;
> given individual and specific instruction directed toward strengths and weaknesses;
> systematically recognized for their achievement (I live in a community where the high school football games are broadcast on prime-time TV).

The Sisk report prompted educators to reexamine two other complex thinking patterns: *leadership* (or human-relations skills) and *creativity*. These patterns are now included in all comprehensive definitions of giftedness.

Leadership is very hard to define. Sometimes the best we can do is agree that Lincoln had it and Snow White didn't. One definition suggested by Dr. Bryan Lindsay is that a gifted leader is anyone who:

> is able to effect (through persuasion and interpersonal communication) positive and productive change;

is able to make decisions;
possesses the personality characteristics known as empathy, sensitivity, proficiency, and charisma.[32]

And if any of us knew what that really was, we could bottle it and sell it off the back of a truck.

For a working concept, we can identify as a gifted leader that individual who:

can become elected president of the Garden Club;
can see that someone of her/his choosing is elected club president;
can control the Garden Club regardless of who's president;
can actually change the blooming seasons.

Chapter 4 will explore the category of creativity in detail, but for now those individuals who are creatively gifted include:

the office clown;
that biologist deep within the bowels of Frito-Lay who's busily cross-breeding carbohydrates unable to adhere to the human digestive tract;
the thespian who revises the community theater's script to "Eddie Puss Wrecks";
anyone who understands at least half of what Robin Williams is talking about;
anyone who decorates a mailbox with something other than woodland fowl.

The Renzulli/Hartman Scale

The second major attempt to organize traits of gifted children is the Renzulli/Hartman Scale for Rating Behavioral Characteristics of Superior Students.[33]

Constructed in 1971, the Renzulli/Hartman Scale was the compilation of research results from over fifty educational projects. It directs teachers to look for student behavior in general learning skills, motivation, creativity, leadership, and planning skills, as well as in artistic, musical, communication, and dramatic abilities.

Read the following excerpts from the Renzulli/Hartman
Scale. Then ask yourself if you too display these behavioral
characteristics.

Learning Skills
- The use of large amounts of data in a variety of subjects
- Quick mastery of information and recall of facts
- Rapid insight into cause-and-effect relationships
- A grasp of underlying principles
- Keen observation skills
- Voracious reading
- Separation of complicated concepts into subcomponents

Motivation
- Reasoning and common sense
- Concentration and absorption in tasks
- Boredom with routine tasks
- Perfectionism
- Preference for independent work
- Assertive or aggressive personality (stubborn in beliefs)
- Judgmental personality
- Preference for detail and organization

Creativity
- Intense curiosity
- Tenacity
- Risk taking
- Sense of humor
- Nonconformity
- A radical and spirited approach to disagreements
- Sensitivity to aesthetics
- Awareness of and openness to impulse
- Hostility toward authority

Leadership
- Responsibility
- Self-confidence
- Popularity among peers
- A cooperative attitude
- Good verbal skills

- Adaptive skills
- A gregarious personality
- A dominant personality
- A preference for group activities

As you reviewed this list and the one prepared by the U.S. Office of Education, you may have concluded that definitions of giftedness and potential genius include every behavior except pretending to be a tree stump. Such a conclusion is absolutely correct. In the "Lost Genius" Self-Evaluation you gained 90 bonus points for detecting the fraudulent test item: "I watch PBS more often than any other TV channel." This is because genius is not a matter of taste; it is a matter of intensity. Genius can occur in *any* subject area. "Certifiable geniuses" have even been known to chuckle at the allegorical content of "The A-Team."

Reading about the ways to sharpen your thinking and learning skills won't make you more tolerant or even prevent Norman Bates from ripping open your shower curtain. But it will show you how to be smarter than you may have ever thought possible.

2

IQ

The Dragon Lives

If you still think an IQ score defines your intelligence, it's time that you gave it another thought. Like a dragon, the IQ is largely a creation of faith, fear, and fantasy. The entire concept fails as an acceptable definition of adult intelligence because:

- The IQ measures simple rather than complex thinking skills.
- The IQ has been a pernicious tool for the discrimination of both individuals and social/cultural groups.
- Since you can learn to score a higher IQ, it does not fulfill its primary promise—the prediction of an innate capacity to think.

Despite such flaws, widespread use of IQ and aptitude tests continues. The reasons for this are partly mercantile: selling intelligence tests is very big business. Not surprisingly, the greatest enthusiasm for and verification of these instruments come from those who market them. But the people who buy the tests—the personnel directors, and psychologists—do so because of something called *hope*. Anyone who stands before a class of students, a group of new employees, or a ward of patients inevitably comes to the same conclusion: "If some standardized formula or insight will reveal the levels at which these people can function, then I can make better decisions about what to do with them." The flaws in the instrument are ignored in the passion of this buoyant expectation.

The concept also survives because those six to eight basic tasks addressed by IQ and aptitude tests are indeed *valid foundation skills*. And there is nothing wrong with being absolutely brilliant in valid foundation skills. In fact, understanding assumptions upon which the tests are constructed—learning how to play the game—can take you one step further toward nurturing more complex, adult intelligence. Let's look more closely at this paradox of failure and survival.

IQ: THE PARADOX

The IQ Measures Simple Rather Than Complex Thinking Skills

To begin with, there's no such thing as *the* IQ test. Over two hundred intelligence tests are now on the market, and new ones are being written every year. Each claims to be the definitive standard for measuring intellectual prowess.

Most IQ tests (and their slightly more sophisticated spawn, the aptitude tests) include elements of:

Vocabulary recognition
Reading comprehension (including factual and inferred data)
Simple verbal reasoning (logic)
Arithmetic and/or algebra
Numerical reasoning (including number sequences and patterns)
Simple figural/abstract reasoning (alterations of form and shape)

There are also three controversial and quasi test skills: short-term memory, the following of directions, and reaction time. They're controversial because educators and psychologists disagree, even among themselves, about whether these elements should be on an intelligence test. They're *quasi* because although they are no longer presented as official test questions (formerly, test takers were asked to listen to and then repeat from memory a series of digits or letters), these three elements still remain significant factors of each and every IQ-type test.

Each intelligence test uses a different scoring mechanism. A numerical *high* on one test could be an *almost high* on a second. Smart test interpreters take the safe ground by issuing the IQ as a range, with so-called normal intelligence falling between 95 and 115. They insist that scores from differing tests should not be interchanged or bandied about. Of course, this hasn't stopped the rest of us from doing it.

A brief history of intelligence testing shows us how the numbers can become so easily muddled.

The first IQ test was conceived for use with children, not adults. In 1905, Alfred Binet, a psychologist and appointee of the French Ministry of Education, collaborated with Theodore Simon, a physician, to construct the first standardized test of intelligence. They wanted to differentiate those children unable to perform simple mental functions from those who were "simply lazy or apathetic."[1] The test was given individually and consisted of buttoning clothing, obeying simple commands, knowing left from right, repeating digits, naming objects, and comparing the lengths of lines.[2] (Why the gentlemen never suspected that lazy and apathetic children would also be lazy and apathetic toward the test has escaped historic record.)

The first Binet test of intelligence (and its early translations) represented scores by a mental age (MA). If you were ten years old and accomplished the tasks determined appropriate for a ten-year-old, all was simple: your MA was ten.

The problems with using MA seemed to occur as American psychologists using the early tests couldn't reconcile the mathematical inconsistencies when: (a) a twenty-year-old scored the same as the ten-year-olds, or (b) a five-year-old scored the same as the ten-year-olds. None of this fit the formula. When an educator hears that statement her response is usually, "So what? Just adapt the lesson plan for individual needs." But these early testers were not constructing lesson plans, they were looking for innate intelligence levels.

Their solution became the IQ score. The first IQs were a ratio of those *correct* answers an individual selected to those same answers selected by the majority of respondents of a specific age. If you were 10 and the number of your correct answers corresponded to the number of correct answers given by the majority of 8-year-olds, your mental age (8) was divided by your chronological age (10) and multiplied by 100 (fractions were cumbersome) to equal an IQ of 80.

Let's look for a moment at what the early test makers meant by a *correct* answer. Correct did not mean "the one true, straight-from-the-lips-of-God answer." Rather, a correct answer was a mathematical necessity—a starting point in the formula for scoring. Specifically, it was the one answer for each question that test writers *predicted* would be selected by most test respondents. Obviously, this system can harbor a "correct" answer that is factually "wrong."

Yet another key element of these tests gives us reason to ponder: the actual mechanics of the test were never intended to measure *adult* success and accomplishment. Even the current Stanford-Binet ratio operates on a mathematical assumption that mental age shrinks in direct proportion to increased chronological age. That is to say, an assumption that more mental development takes place in early years. (Remember Piaget?) The difference, therefore, between the test's mental age for 5-year-old accomplishment and 6-year-old accomplishment is much greater than is the difference between the mental age for 20-year-old accomplishment and 21-year-old accomplishment. On the Stanford-Binet IQ test, for example, adults rarely register much beyond a mental age of 15 years and 9 months.[3]

Even the so-called adult-level tests merely utilize more difficult vocabulary to present the same simple tasks. And all IQ and aptitude tests exclude significant aspects of adult intelligence, such as: complex deductive reasoning, the development of personal values and judgments, problem-solving skills (particularly when elements of the problem—unlike tests and puzzles—are not completely revealed), interpersonal communication skills, and creativity.

There is one very valid reason for ignoring these aspects of adult intelligence: constructing a test that elicits, evaluates, and then measures all intellectual components of even the most simple real-life problem would be an incredible challenge. Test makers, therefore, must postulate that anyone who can reason within a very confined set of cues or circumstances will be able to reason in other, more complex circumstances.

Unfortunately, removing complexity from a test is not easy. And when a test item is successfully simplified to a *testable* and *statistically verifiable* format, that action in itself creates new testing problems:

- Without intimidation and the threat of eternal damnation to stupidity, the test can be incredibly boring.
  Clouds always appear when it rains.
  It is raining now.
  Therefore, what must be true?

(Several researchers have concluded that it is the high-ability reader who most often fails or refuses to comprehend poorly constructed or boring reading material.[4])

- Because simpler test questions contain fewer cues, your chances of hitting upon the winning answer can actually *decrease* unless you and the test writer agree 100 percent upon all interpretations of every word. (Enter the threat of cultural bias.)

But assuming you comprehend the test question; assuming you and the test writer agree upon all cues; and assuming you do indeed have *some* basic reasoning skills, you can still miss an answer if:

- You are so *highly skilled* at reasoning that you identify original insights to the problem that were not apparent to the test writer and thus not within the list of solution alternatives. In short: you could be creative. And creative thinkers are penalized on a test requiring selection of the *one true* answer!

The first standardized intelligence test was a noble effort, based in the belief that mentally retarded children could be singled out and taught to be more intelligent. It is indeed a tragedy that Binet's primary motivation was totally ignored by his immediate predecessors. Joseph O. Loretan, the head of the New York City Board of Education, which suspended IQ testing for its students, stated, "[After Binet's] death psychologists suggested [intelligence was] an inherited, general mental quality susceptible to accurate and easy measurement."[5] And Dr. Leon Kamin remarked, "It is perhaps as well that Binet died in 1911 before witnessing the uses to which his test was speedily put in the United States."[6]

IQ and Aptitude Tests Discriminate Against the Individual and the Group

IQ tests discriminate first and foremost against people who have not learned test-taking skills. Everyone recognizes that a standardized test can be negatively affected by test anxiety, environmental distractions, physical illness, emotional trauma unrelated to the test, and inaccurate or incompetent test instructions. (I have very clear memories of my own seventh-grade encounter with incompetent test instructions. The teacher set a windup kitchen timer to the allotted interval and proceeded to read us the test instructions. Even *then* I knew *that* wasn't right.) If you haven't learned to control distractions or compensate for the errors of others—you lose. Furthermore, the standardized language and verbal cues within test instructions favor the experienced test taker. It helps, for example, if you know that in the figural analogy △ ◆ △: □ ◆ ? the symbol (:) means *in the same relationship as* and that the figure (◆) means "Look to where this arrow is pointing." This point may seem trivial now, but you can eat up a lot of time on the figural analogies of a more sophisticated aptitude test when

trying to remember the exact meanings of mathematical codes
such as cos, <,>, sin, [], △, /, °, etc. You may have excelled at
an IQ or aptitude test *not* because you were genetically pre-
determined to do so, but because you were practiced in those
specific skills the test measured.

Not one psychological text or educational journal of the
last quarter century equates IQ with total intelligence. Not
one. When Moses received the tablets, IQ was not even a point
of discussion. Yet many people maintain a reverent assumption
that this single score measures how smart they *really* are.
These individuals can experience a deep sense of defeat when
an IQ test score falls short of their expectations. Many people
overcome this feeling by achieving success as adults, but for
the individual whose entire social, ethnic, and cultural identity
group fails the test, such achievement can be more difficult. We
cannot ignore the fact that the IQ has often been used as a tool
of widespread social discrimination. The first American test
writers/marketers, Drs. Lewis Terman, Robert Yerkes, and
Henry Goddard, had publicly proclaimed the genetic determination of intelligence and the superiority of the intelligence
level of one race over all others (guess which one).[7]

Widespread discrimination began when World War I
prompted the prostitution of Binet's test for retarded children
into a tool of troop deployment. Hundreds of thousands of task
assignments required decisions in response to questions such
as: "Is this guy smart enough to lead a battalion?" "Should that
guy be helping us with military strategy, or should he be a tar-
get for artillery practice?" You don't have to be a mathemati-
cian to see how military-deployment specialists deduced a
direct correlation between a recruit's high IQ score and his distance from the front line.

But the greatest social injustice came after the war when
a no-doubt well-intentioned bureaucrat decided to use the
Army intelligence tests for a little crowd control on Ellis Island. These tests (the Alpha—for literate, English-speaking
adults —and the Beta—for illiterate and/or non-English-speak-
ing adults) contained items such as:

The Brooklyn Nationals are called the:
a. Giants   **b.** Orioles   **c.** Superbas   **d.** Indians
Revolvers are made by:
a. Swift & Co.   **b.** Smith & Wesson   **c.** W. L. Douglas
d. B. T. Babbitt[8]

Knowing about baseball and handguns was certainly no sin. But IQ scores resulting from such test questions were subsequently used by federal immigration committees to determine how many individuals of each specific ethnic and national group would be allowed into this country. Even more sobering are the hundreds of reports from refugees and immigration officials that the Alpha and Beta were routinely interchanged.[9]

The worldwide outcry against this kind of cultural bias began in 1923 when the London Board of Education issued a stern warning that the Stanford-Binet discriminated against "underpriviledged, isolated and often illiterate children of English canal-boat families" (their *average* IQ score was 69.9).[10]

The outcry continued in 1964 with the publication of the "Guidelines for Testing Minority Group Children," which showed how even nonverbal questions can be subject to cultural bias.[11] In one very popular intelligence test, children had been shown a picture of a teacup and asked to match it to a picture of either: **a.** saucer, **b.** dog, **c.** table, or **d.** shoe. Researchers found that inner-city, rural, and some groups of foreign-born children rarely matched cup to saucer, as the college educated, middle-class test designers had intended. These children most often saw a cup sitting on a bare table. And their observations were scored as *incorrect*.

More recently, Stephen Jay Gould in his book *The Mismeasure of Man* condemned the IQ as a device that continues to perpetuate the idea that intelligence is genetic, and therefore more prevalent (or absent) in specific races or cultures.[12]

I stated earlier that IQ survives because of a hope that it can predict a student's future lifetime success. Tragically, no data conclusively support this position.[13] Even those most inflated claims of predictability extend only to success in the most

simple of scholastic/academic tasks: reading, recalling, and re-
gurgitating.

In the journal *American Psychologist*, D. C. McClelland
asks, "Why should intelligence or aptitude tests have all this
power? What justifies the use of such tests in selecting applicants for college entrance or jobs? On what assumption is the
movement based?"[14] If you now believe that a past IQ score
represents your *real* intelligence, you should ask yourself this
very question.

Multiple-Aptitude Batteries, or What to Do after Everybody Learns How to Work Simple IQ Tests

World War II and its ensuing troop-deployment problems
resulted in new ways of approaching intelligence testing. Psychologists now began to emphasize aptitude profiles rather
than IQ measurement, in the hopes that overall ratings of an
individual's strengths and weaknesses would be more reveal-
ing than a single score.

The aptitude battery has become the most common tool of
educational evaluation, while the simple IQ test is used more
often in clinical settings. Yet well-known multiple-aptitude
batteries—the Scholastic Aptitude Test, Graduate Record Examination, and the Law School Admissions Test—evolved directly from the Stanford-Binet. The SAT changed its name,
refined its table manners, and moved uptown. Instead of the
old IQ, scores range from 200 to 800 with a norm at about 500.
But once an S-B, always an S-B. The verbal portions of the test
still contain vocabulary, analogies, sentence completion, and
comprehension, and we find Stanford-Binet's numerical reasoning, plus an additional helping of algebra, in the quantitative sections. While IQ and aptitude tests have countless
minute differences, they vary significantly only as to the test-
er's purpose for accumulating data.[15]

Aptitude test results are issued in a complex mathematical
analysis called the *factor matrix*. In this format, subtest components of your responses to each test question are weighed

and compared. Finally you are told relative values of your proficiency areas and functional age levels. The concept of multiple aptitude was an important step beyond the idea of measuring general intelligence by a single score. But unfortunately it never gained popular support. Not even a genius can walk away from such an intellectual diagnostic session with anything as tidy as the IQ to tuck into his mental hip pocket.

Teaching IQ Skills

Almost anyone can be taught to score higher on an IQ test. Such training projects have usually focused on children, but the results are applicable to all age groups.

In 1964, researchers at the University of Wisconsin set about to study and train a group of Milwaukee infants born to mothers who showed no signs of brain disease or trauma, but who had IQs of less than 75. The long-term training program consisted of language-development classes, verbal-expression exercises, reading, mathematics, and basic problem solving. In addition, the mothers received instruction in homemaking, baby-care skills, and, when possible, vocational training. After the test period, the average IQ of the trained children was 124 with a single high of 135.[16] Such scores constitute gifted intelligence by anybody's definition.

A University of Illinois study exposed small groups of nursery-school children to intensive math concepts, language arts, reading readiness, and science, raising their scores an average of 8 points on the Stanford-Binet. In a replication of the study, other students made gains of 12 to 14 points.[17] (Even teachers get better with practice.)

Scholars at the University of Illinois took part in several similar training programs and reported IQ gains of 15 points and achievement test scores of approximately one year above age norms.[18]

In a study at Albert Einstein College of Medicine, preschoolers were tutored for 15 to 20 minutes each day. Group Stanford-Binet scores rose from an average of 97.7 to 112.2.[19]

Children in the New York City Demonstration Guidance

Project gained an average of 8 points in their IQs during a 1956–57 experiment, while scores in 1959–60 rose an average of 15 IQ points. The most dramatic gain came from a student whose IQ leaped 40 points after training.[20]

And, finally, a 1965 West Point study of intense SAT preparatory training programs at ten high schools showed that SAT test scores were improved an average of 136 points as a direct result of training.[21]

Such gains would not have been possible if IQ were indeed an innate and measurable commodity accompanying you from womb to tomb.

"Intelligence tests" have a very specific and limited function. Nevertheless, practicing IQ skills[22] can help you reach greater sophistication in:

- Recognizing and recalling words and verbal relationships;
- Recognizing patterns by which figural images can change;
- Approaching both verbal and figural problems with a mind open to *atypical* solutions.

ELEMENTS OF MODERN IQ/APTITUDE TESTS

Since there are hundreds of available intelligence tests, any single test could contain any number of specific question categories. The most commonly seen are:

Figural Problems
Figural comprehension
　Figural classification
Spatial comprehension
Complex figural completion
Spatial reasoning (logic)
　Blocks
　Reflected images

Arithmetic and algebra
Figural reasoning (logic)
   Series completion
      Simple figural series
      Complex figural series
   Figural analogies
   Figural matrices

Verbal Problems
Word recognition
   Definitions
   Synonyms
   Antonyms
Verbal comprehension (both factual and inferred)
   Sentence comprehension
   Paragraph comprehension
   Complex verbal comprehension
Verbal deductive reasoning (logic)
   Verbal series completion
   Sentence completion
   Verbal analogies
   Syllogisms
   Complex deductive puzzles

Taming the Dragon

LEARNING IQ SKILLS

The following problems have been constructed to illustrate those you may have encountered in past IQ and aptitude tests. Some are simple; others seem unfair and puzzling. As you approach each, remember the following formula:

    Step 1   Read instructions carefully.
    Step 2   Break the problem into its simplest parts.
    Step 3   Work the easiest subproblem first.

Figural Problems

Okay—I'm not afraid to say it—in tests of both mathematical and spatial relationships, males usually outscore females. I've heard feminists answer this by noting that girls usually aren't allowed to climb trees in their party dresses or estimate fifty yards from the middle of a football field. But some of us did climb trees despite the party dress. Many of us didn't even have a party dress. Moreover, many of us *were* given opportunities to judge distances and spatial relationships—if not on the football field, then by judging the distance to the baseline of the opposite court or by setting out cauliflower starts in the family garden.

There are three possible answers:

1. Females cannot physically process the intellectual functions necessary for abstract, figural, and spatial reasoning as well as can males.
2. Females have been given fewer opportunities to learn such processing skills than have males.
3. Females have been told by the specifics of test questions (almost always written by males) and by mathematics in elementary school (almost always presented by females) that those examples of abstract, figural, and spatial reasoning present in "little girl" activities are not the same as *real* mathematics or geometry.

I honestly don't know which answer will eventually be proven correct.[23] I do know what I see, and I have never seen an elementary-school math lesson that began: "Today we're going to learn basic arithmetic, plane geometry, basic algebra, figural analogy, and spatial orientation. Now—I want you all to make an exact copy of this dress—only half scale for Barbie's little sister."

Another physical element of figural test questions affects both males and females. Spatial problems on IQ/aptitude tests usually consist of major geometric forms: lines, squares, circles, triangles, etc.—an obvious fact when you consider the two-dimensional limitations of paper and ink. More advanced blocks and shading have been incorporated in an attempt to replicate three dimensions, but even they seem elementary when compared to real-life mechanical problem solving. (A series of three-dimensional "mechanical aptitude tests" have evolved, primarily in business and industry, but such tests are expensive to produce and administer and so rarely make their way into the junior-high test battery.)

The physical limitations of IQ/aptitude tests even influence the content of school curricula. Educational practice has always tended to follow *popular test skills* as if stapled to the animal's tail. Verbal skills are more easily facilitated by standardized testing instruments. Therefore, most schoolchildren receive only cursory instruction in complex three-dimensional spatial and figural problem solving until they are old enough to select specialty areas such as higher mathematics, vocational arts, and fine arts.

But change is in the air. Soon all IQ/aptitude and achievement tests will be administered at the computer terminal. And this instrument is far superior to the 8½-x-11-inch booklet and number-2 pencil when presenting abstract and figural reasoning. This will mean more elaborate figural test items, and thus the teaching of more complex spatial and abstract concepts— an educational revolution.

Meanwhile, the steps for solving any two-dimensional figural problem remain relatively straightforward:

> ***Step 1***   Recognize primary geometric forms.
> ***Step 2***   Identify changes.

Dr. Robert Sternberg discovered that those individuals who score the highest on spatial problems (male or female) are more adept at this second step.[24] Change can occur in any number of ways—but the most common changes are:[25]

A Reversal:

Size Alteration:

Alteration in Shading:

Shape Alteration (often in combination with shading):

Rotation (clockwise or counterclockwise):

Addition or Deletion:

Separation of All Parts:

Bonding of All Parts:

Movement of Only One Part:

Visual/spatial skills can influence and even—in the case of dyslexia or myopia—hinder other types of intellectual processing. In the absence of physical impairment, however, the most efficient method for increasing your visual/spatial orientation skills continues to be practice.

As you approach visual/spatial problems, follow this adaptation of the general game plan:

> ***Step 1*** Look for the simplest problem first.
>
> ***Step 2*** Identify major components of each figure. Then trace or reproduce each element. This reinforces key images and serves the same purpose as repeating a verbal problem out loud.
>
> ***Step 3*** Note any changes. Make a list. This is where Macho Math can be your downfall; who says you must work all such problems in your head?
>
> ***Step 4*** Apply these changes to the unknowns. Hypothesize, test, rule out blind alleys.

Figural Comprehension

Figural Classification

Find the figure that should go with the others.

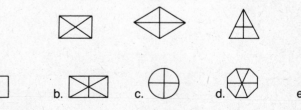

Answer

Look for the most obvious similarity between the three figures. They are different shapes, but each contains two intersecting lines. The only other figure of any shape containing two such lines is **c**.

Spatial Comprehension.

If put together, the shapes below will form what larger shape?

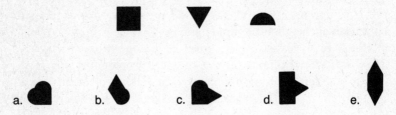

a.   b.   c.   d.   e.

Answer

c. Anyone who's ever made a birthday cake in the shape of a chicken's head would have spotted it in a flash.

Spatial Reasoning (Logic)

Spatial reasoning includes problems such as blocks and reflected images.

Blocks

How many blocks are in each figure?

1. 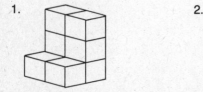   2.

Each of the following blocks is identically lettered with A, B, C, and D. Two sides are blank. What letters are hidden from view on each block and in what order do the letters appear, left to right?

3.

4. Which side (letter) is fully touching side A?

5. Which letter is opposite side D?

Reflected Images

In each series below, underline the pair of figures representing reflected (mirror) images.

(Your skill in handling this puzzle is determined by your understanding of the phrase *reflected image*. Imagine placing a mirror against either the bottom or side of the figure. What second figure is seen in the reflection?)

1.

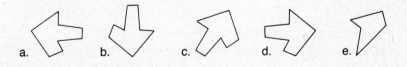

a.   b.   c.   d.   e.

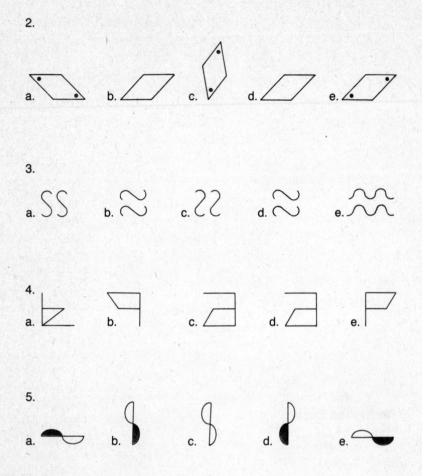

2.

3.

4.

5.

Answers

Blocks:

    1. 8   **2.** 4   **3.** left block: B, A; right block: C, B   **4.** B   **5.** B

Reflected images:

    1. a., d.   **2. a., e.** Did you spot the duplicates, **b.** and

d.? These are not "mirror images."   **3. a., c.**   **4. b.,
e.   5. b., d.**

Figural Reasoning (Logic)

Series Completion

Simple Figural Series   These problems can be simple
patterns of form or number. But they can also involve a combination of a verbal symbol *and* a simple pattern. Several researchers have categorized the types of letter patterns used in
these series problems. These include:

> Simple patterns (no verbal meaning):
>   letter pairs: tall/bell
>   vowel/consonant groupings: beat/peat
>   numerical relationships: 1, 2, 3, 4
> Pattern plus verbal meaning:
>   word constructions: mangrove/potholder

1. What figure would come next in this series?

Answer
    ☐ It is a change in form and shading.

2. Which two numbers come next?

         5   1   6   2   7   3   ?   ?

Answers
    8, 4. These things can get quite vicious. Supposedly you've
been given enough clues to enable you to guess the series relationship. But once again, creativity is a handicap.
    Actually there are two ways to solve this problem. The
most obvious is the completion of a diagram charting mathematical relationships.

The difference between numbers, i.e., the difference between 5 and 1 is (-4).

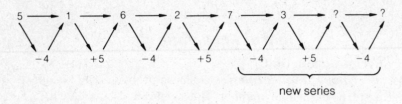

new series

Note the beginning of a new series (-4), ($+5$), (-4), etc., and apply the mathematics in reverse.

This technique serves us well when the problem is simple, and it is by far the more popular of the two. But the second technique becomes more relevant in larger, adult problem-solving situations. Try looking for more creative perspectives. Then you may notice that there are actually two alternating series within this problem:

$$5 \quad 1 \quad 6 \quad 2 \quad 7 \quad 3 \quad ? \quad ?$$
$$* \quad - \quad * \quad - \quad * \quad - \quad * \quad -$$

3. Which letter comes next in the following series?

F   S   S   M   T   W   ?

a. F   b. M   c. S   d. T   e. W

Answer

   d. This question is a combination of the symbol or meaning of each letter and its pattern or sequence in the series. T stands for Thursday since this series represents the days of the week. Now don't get angry with me if you made it more complicated than it really was. It could have been worse: I could have placed them out of their usually presented pattern *and* not given you any multiple choice.

   Once again we see the phenomenon of educational bias.

Many of us have been taught to attack this kind of problem with mathematics—the simple pattern. As in the previous example we look at the numbers or letters and try to devise some mathematical formula for breaking the code: "Let's see, the third letter is 4 alphabetic places away from the second and 7 less than the fourth. . . ." But, since these kinds of problems can also be a series utilizing the verbal symbol (or meaning) of a word or letter *in addition to* the figural pattern, the best strategy is to step back from the problem and look at the big picture. Learning such open-mindedness may be one of the most valuable lessons of the IQ/aptitude test.

There is a puzzle of this sort on a screening test given Mensa aspirants:[26]

The figures below represent a code. Decipher the code and form as many words as possible out of the letters.

Give up?

When I showed this problem to my eight-year-old, he said, "Oh yeah. That's that *news* thing."

The arrows represent North-East-West-South and he'd seen the puzzle in the *Electric Company* children's magazine.

Case closed.

Complex Figural Series The system seen in question 2 (page 47) still works with more complex number problems. For example:

$$13 \quad 15 \quad 14 \quad 16 \quad ? \quad 17$$

The difference between

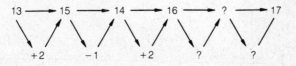

At this point you could guess at a pattern $+2-1+2-1$ and complete the problem with $16 - 1 = 15$ and $15 + 2 = 17$. If you still weren't secure about guessing (or if the pattern weren't as obvious as $+2-1+2-1$) you could continue the matrix.

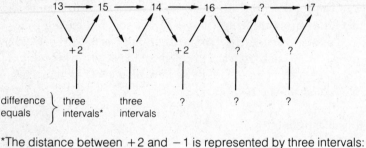

*The distance between $+2$ and -1 is represented by three intervals: $+2$, $+1$, 0 and -1.

Now, even though your sample is small (only two numbers), you do have a consistent pattern: three intervals. Try plugging in the numbers, remembering that a three-interval relationship with $+2$ can either be $+5$ or -1.

Taking the worst case first:

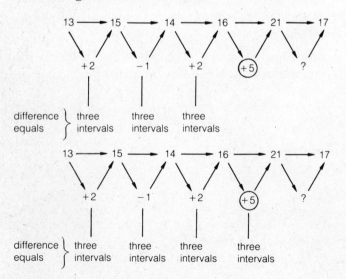

Now the relationship for the new ? could equal 2 or 8. But neither 21 + 2 nor 21 + 8 equals the next number in the series: 17. Five does not complete the series. Back to the drawing board with our second alternative answer: (− 1).

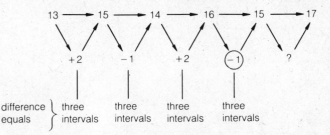

Possible alternatives for (?) are +2 and (− 4): 15 + 2 = 17. And 15 + (− 4) does not. See how handy it is to take a chance and guess early in the game?

Try your hand at the practice problems below. Don't forget the rules:

- Look first to the big picture and try to identify any *physical patterns*.
- Apply the solution pattern illustrated above.

1. 9   22   35   ?   61

2. 97   85   ?   61   49   37

3. 14   17   23   ?   44   59

4. 19   28   36   45   54   ?   82   91

Answers

1. 48. Pattern is +13.   **2.** 73. Pattern is (− 12). **3.** 32. Pattern is + multiples of 3 (+ 3, + 6, + 9, etc.).   **4.** 63. Did you forget the *big picture*? Start at each end and reverse the digits.

In another type of complex figural problem, a series is completed by changing the position, number, scale, and/or shading of the figures and their parts.

What figure comes next in the series?

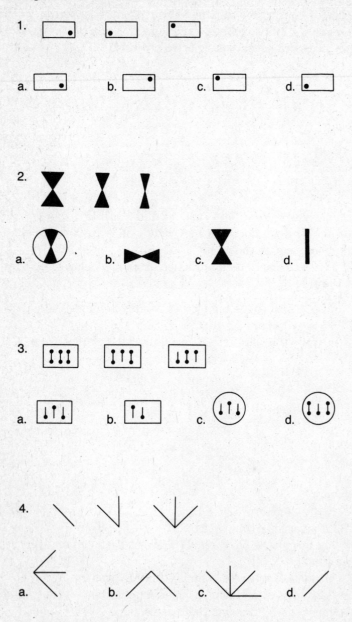

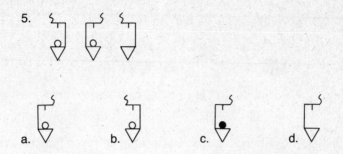

5.

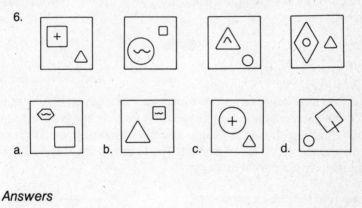

a.   b.   c.   d.

Another kind of configuration problem: Which figure belongs with these?

6.

a.   b.   c.   d.

Answers

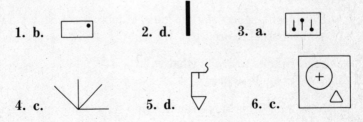

1. b.   2. d.   3. a.

4. c.   5. d.   6. c.

Figural Analogies

In an analogous statement you are to deduce a relationship for **c** to **d** that is identical to the relationship existing between

a and **b.** Look at the following:

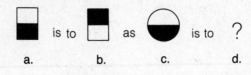

a.   b.   c.   d.

Begin by analyzing the relationship between figures **a** and **b.** Both geometric forms are the same, but in figure **b** the shading has moved from the bottom section to the top section. Therefore, to construct figure **d** you reproduce the same geometric form seen in figure **c** and move the shading from the bottom to the top section:

As a means of cross-reference, we can apply a general rule for solving analogies. It is: If you can't identify the relationship of **a** to **b,** find the relationship of **a** to **c.** Then apply that same relationship to a **b** and **d** pairing. The principle may be easier to discern with a verbal analogy:

steel is to *ceramic* as *ore* is to ?

If you can't see a relationship of steel to ceramic, try a relationship of steel to ore.

Steel relates to ore in what way?
Steel is made of ore.

Now apply this same relationship to ceramic and the unknown:

Ceramic is made of what?
Clay.
Therefore, steel is to ceramic as ore is to clay.

Here is another example:

Los Angeles is to *California* as *Burbank* is to ?
a. Burbank   **b.** California   **c.** Los Angeles   **d.** USA

Los Angeles is to Burbank in what way?
Los Angeles includes Burbank.

Substituting California for Los Angeles, we see that California includes two answers—Burbank and Los Angeles. But since Burbank can't occupy both **c** and **d** slots (Los Angeles and California are not the same—honest), the correct answer is Los Angeles.

Los Angeles is to California as Burbank is to Los Angeles.

Now apply the rule to a complex figural analogy containing more than one element of change. For example:

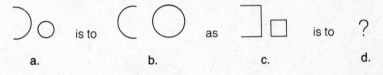

  a.   **b.**   **c.**   **d.**

Analyze the relationship of **a** to **c**. Figure **a** is a big arc pointing left, with a little circle; figure **c** is a big bracket pointing left, with a little square. Thus the relationship is a change in categories (curved lines to straight lines). The pattern for these particular categories is: big sections pointing the same way, followed by like and smaller wholes. (Would I lie?)

Now look at the pattern of figure **b**. It is a large arc pointing right, followed by a large circle. The change in categories would make figure **d** a large bracket pointing right, followed by a large square.

There are some figural and verbal analogies for which the rule does not apply. They are ones in which the relationship of **a** to **b** is far more apparent than is any relationship of **a** to **c**. For example:

Cream is to *butter* as *wheat* is to ?
Cream is to wheat as ? That *is* rather opaque; just concentrate on the
a-to-**b** relationship.

Another example:

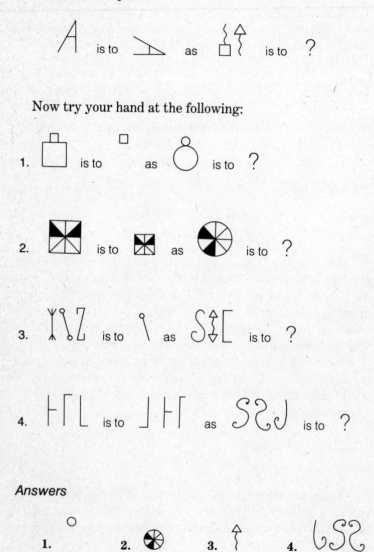

Now try your hand at the following:

1.   is to   as   is to   ?

2.   is to   as   is to   ?

3.   is to   as   is to   ?

4.   is to   as   is to   ?

Answers

1.   2.   3.   4.

Figural Matrices

The Latin Square   Often found on adult IQ tests, this figural puzzle is intended to evaluate your ability to spot relationships among elements of a complex design. First devised in 1938 by two English psychologists, the problem consists of nine squares, eight of which contain one of three different figures. The inherent *rules* of the puzzle dictate that each of the three appears once in each row and each column. You are to deduce the ninth figure.

A simple Latin square would be as follows:

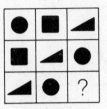

When the figures are three simple geometric forms, one glance to the puzzle is often enough to spot the missing figure (in this case, a square). But what about something a little more complex? Like:

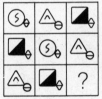

Two English educators, David Lewis and James Greene, have devised a simple mathematical technique for quickly solving such problems:[27]

- Check the two figures in the diagonal containing the empty square.
- If they are identical, the missing figure is the same.
- If they are different, the missing figure is identical to the figure above the center box.

Test the Lewis/Greene formula by working the following Latin square exercises:

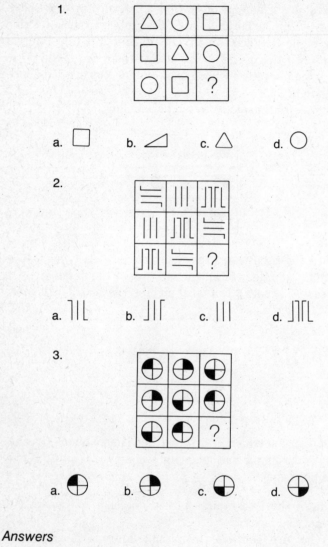

1.

a. ☐   b. ◺   c. △   d. ◯

2.

a. ⊺⊺∟   b. ⊿⊺⌐   c. ⊺⊺⊺   d. ⌐⊺∟

3.

a. ⊕   b. ⊕   c. ⊕   d. ⊕

Answers
  1. c.   2. c.   3. b.

Multiple Variance Matrix A second, more sophisticated form of matrix problem has been known to drive even the
most stalwart puzzle genius to strong drink. In this problem,
all *rules* are abandoned as the missing figure can be totally dissimilar to any of the other eight figures. You must detect a pattern of change and deduce the figure that probably completes
the series.

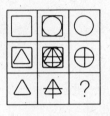

a. b. c. d.

Answer
   d.

Try to complete the following matrices.

1.

a. b. c. d.

2.

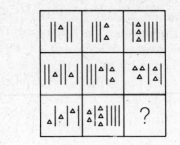

a. ‖‖‖△△   b. |△|△|△|△|△|△| c. △|△‖|△| d. △‖

3.

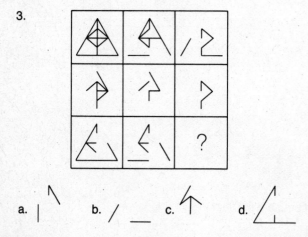

a. |⌐   b. /—   c. 个   d. ∠

Answers

1.   **c.**   Reading left to right in the horizontal rows, we see the top of a figure, the bottom of a figure, and the total figure in a circle. Reading top to bottom in the vertical rows we see all tops, all bottoms, all wholes in circles. (Wholes in circles being a very neat trick.)

2.   **b.**   Concentrate on the triangles, not the entire figure. In both horizontal and vertical rows we see a definite increase in the number of triangles. Now look to the lines; all we

can tell about the lines is that no number of lines is repeated.
But this is a pattern too. So look to the answer that contains an
increase in triangles and a dissimilar number of lines.

3. b. This is the one that used to make my eyes cross on
those old college-entrance exams. Actually, it's rather simple if
someone shows you how it was constructed.

Chart the elements of the most complex figure in the matrix (in this case, the upper left corner). The figure consists of
sixteen segments:

A	B	C
D	E	F
G	H	I

Look for a relationship between blocks A, B, and C. B and
C appear to contain elements of the figure in block A. Label
each segment so that it corresponds to its *duplicate* within
block A.

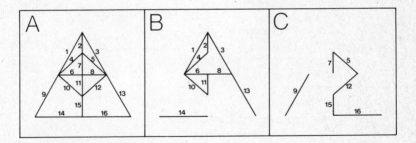

Eureka! There's a blatant pattern! The figures in blocks B
and C combine to form the figure in block A. If you look again
to the original puzzle, you will see that the same pattern exists
in the relationships of A, D, and G; D, E, and F; C, F, and I,

etc. When you know the trick, solving this puzzle is much simpler than stretching your paycheck or keeping ahead of your favorite enemy. And yet a lot of people equate such puzzle-solving skills with genius.

Verbal Problems

Word Recognition

The purpose of this kind of test question is to identify your exposure to specific (and random) vocabulary, your understanding of each word, and, to a general degree, your retention of words.

Definitions

Find the best definition for each italicized word.

1. *circumscribe*
   a. a surgical procedure
   b. to encircle
   c. an event
   d. a letter of complaint
   e. a hesitant circus reporter
2. *modular*
   a. in fashion
   b. modern
   c. a state of calmness
   d. an announcer
   e. a small unit of measurement
3. *cosmo*
   a. a character in the old TV series "Topper"
   b. the title of a magazine
   c. world
   d. an Italian singer
   e. something to do with Carl Sagan

Answers

1. b.   2. e.   3. c. Fooled you. With a lower-case letter, the word means "world." Anything else (even with an **s**) would have had a capital *C*.

Synonyms

In each, find the word that means the same as the italicized word.

1. *announcement*
   a. stage fright
   b. greeting card
   c. proclamation
   d. microphone
   e. "Whoever has the blue Ford, your lights are on."
2. *convexity*
   a. seersucker
   b. magnum
   c. bulge
   d. talisman
   e. ear
3. *continuance*
   a. bookmark
   b. cessation
   c. jail sentence
   d. "Your place or mine? Waiter, check, please!"
   e. extension
4. *shuffle*
   a. stand, stamp
   b. establish
   c. alter
   d. a transport at Disney World
   e. cater
5. *concord*
   a. variance
   b. homology
   c. cenotaph
   d. an airplane
   e. petulance
6. *operculum*
   a. magnificence
   b. blemish
   c. the final song in an operatic sequence
   d. a layer of a painted surface
   e. eyelid

Answers
    1. c.   **2. c.**   **3. e.**   **4. c.**   **5. b.**   **6. e.**

Antonyms

Usually these questions require that you simply find the words which are opposite in their literal meaning. But in more sophisticated aptitude tests, this same kind of question can become an exercise in verbal reasoning or logic.

Example: Underline the two words in the following series that are opposite in their meanings.
1. acquisition   transgression   loss   performance   manipulation
2. vindicate   pacify   investigate   punish   ignore
3. stagirite   festoon   reboat   slattern   ululate
4. felicitation   skepticism   exculpation   credulity   concinnity
5. prostrate   loquacious   taciturn   sanguine   enigmatic

Answers
1. acquisition/loss   2. vindicate/punish
3. stagirite/slattern   4. skepticism/credulity
5. loquacious/taciturn

Wish you had the verbal dexterity demonstrated by these problems? Use a Word-a-Day calendar. Don't guess at the meaning of a word; look it up in the dictionary. Buy yourself a thesaurus. The kind of language facility represented here develops only through reading, conversing, and listening to others who are verbally fluent. (That's why your mother always wanted you to be with the "right" crowd.)

Verbal Comprehension (Both Factual and Inferred)

As we've seen, the simplest form of verbal comprehension is the recognition and remembering of vocabulary. But the following exercises direct you toward a more complex task: the evaluation and analysis of written passages.

When seen on an IQ/aptitude test, this kind of comprehension requires that you address both *literal understanding* (word for word) and *inference* (reading between the lines). You must comprehend both the main idea and supporting or secondary ideas (organization patterns). The most commonly used relationships are:

- *Sequential format* (cause and effect). This can be either chronological—step by step according to time—or by order of importance—involving a judgment of least important to most important event, regardless of time. Sequential format is seen most clearly in a representation of a dramatic event, telling of a story, etc.
- *Reverse sequential format* (journalistic format). The most important point first, followed by supporting data.
- *Compare-and-contrast format*. Used most often in written passages that attempt to sell or persuade.

Sentence Comprehension

This type of question often involves a proverb or old saying. For example:

What is meant by the proverb, "The exception proves the rule"?
a. You can't always trust rules.
b. Every rule has an exception.
c. It isn't a real rule without an exception.
d. Rules and exceptions are really the same.

Answer

This question is unfair if you know more than the test constructor anticipated or knew himself. When this proverb was translated from the Latin, *provo* was often misinterpreted as "prove." A more correct translation, however, is *test*. "The exception *tests* the rule."[28] (A moment's celebration for those of you who always reasoned that an exception should have *disproven* a rule.) **c** is the most commonly selected answer (and probably the one most test writers would have meant) since it reinforces what is a basic error in the translated proverb. But, if you knew Latin or if you were creative, you could make a very good case for **a, b,** or **d**! It seems to me to be based entirely upon your philosophical viewpoint.

Read the following sentences and select the best interpretation.

> From hence, ye beauties, undeceived,
> Know, one false step is ne'er retrieved,
>   And be with caution bold.
> Not all that tempts your wandering eyes
> And heedless hearts, is lawful prize;
>   Nor all, that glisters, gold.   —Thomas Gray

    a. There are many beautiful things in life that merely exist to tempt you.

    b. That which you want the most is often the most deceitful.

    c. When you chase goldfish, you could slip in the tub and drown.

    d. You can't always get what you want, so take comfort in the fact that it's rarely as good as it looks anyway.

    e. Be careful what kind of risks you take, because that which you seek may not be as valuable as the price you must ultimately pay.

Answer

Lots of people choose **d** since it resembles the implied meaning of the old saying: "All that glitters is not gold." While such an adage was presumably instructional to the Forty-niners, it has minor significance in this passage. If you had recognized the stanza as coming from "Ode on the Death of a Favorite Cat" you would have known that Thomas Gray was indeed talking about a cat that drowned in a tub of goldfish. Therefore, you might have been momentarily tempted to select **c**. Upon a bit more reflection, however, I'm certain you would have selected **e** as the correct answer. These exercises test your ability to balance literal as well as implied meanings and thus "judge" which is the "best inference." They represent the closest link between test skills and real-life adult problem solving.

Paragraph Comprehension

This is often combined with arithmetic and deductive reasoning to create the beloved story-problem:

    1. You go into a liquor store with three twenties. You spend 1/4 of it for wine, a twenty and a five on Scotch, $10 on mixers, and 10 percent of the original amount on some Beer Nuts. Do you have any money left? If so, how much?

2. Sarah owns a small bookstore. One day a customer buys the $35 leather-bound copy of *Macho Mothers Don't Do Housework* and pays Sarah with a fifty-dollar bill. As the customer is leaving he sees some note cards he also wants to buy (cost: $7.50) and he pays this time with a new twenty-dollar bill. Later Sarah learns that both bills were counterfeit. Both items had been sale priced at the same cost they were to Sarah. Ignoring her costs of overhead, how much did Sarah lose in this transaction?

Answers
1. Yes. $4
2. $70

Such problems, of course, only *look* imposing. Take them as a series of small steps.

three twenties =	$60
wine—1/4 of $60	− 15
	45
Scotch	− 25
	20
mixers	− 10
10 percent of total (.10 × 60)	− 6
	$4 change

P.S. You could get sick on $6 worth of Beer Nuts.

Complex Verbal Comprehension

In a test you are forced to select one of the answer alternatives as being the "most correct." But when you apply the principles of comprehension to a real-life problem, you are not bound by such artificial circumstances. The following comprehension puzzles will help you make the transition from "test thinking" to "adult thinking."

Even complex written (and oral) passages can be interpreted with the following simple formula:

Step 1 Get the main idea.
Step 2 Identify supporting data within the passage.
Step 3 Identify the relationship of ideas.

Step 1   Get the Main Point

Read the following passages and *make a judgment* regarding the
most appropriate title—or main idea—for each.

(In a test situation, you can only *hope* that your judgment
fits one of the answer alternatives. Here, in the safety of your
own book, you can actually create a better one.)

1.   Finally, and most convincingly, in 1822 Goethe himself notes a
strange celestial phenomenon. "En route home from the Leipzig Anxiety Festival," he wrote, "I was crossing a meadow, when I chanced to
look up and saw several fiery red balls suddenly appear in the southern sky. They descended at a great rate of speed and began chasing
me. I screamed that I was a genius and consequently could not run
very fast, but my words were wasted. I became enraged and shouted
imprecations at them, whereupon they flew away frightened. I related
this story to Beethoven, not realizing he had already gone deaf, and
he smiled and nodded and said, 'Right.'"....

—Woody Allen, *Side Effects*[29]

Select the best title:
   a.   "Goethe Pimps Beethoven"
   b.   "Goethe Observes Strange Celestial Phenomenon"
   c.   "Geniuses Can't Run Fast"
   d.   Other:

2.   We have sought to make clear that psychology may be given a
place, as science, alongside of the acknowledged sciences, and we
have sought to justify this adventure by the proof that psychologists
built upon what, in our view, is a non-scientific foundation are contra-
dictory and instable. But we have, of course, no access to any private
store of psychological facts and no short and easy method of adding
to the results of observation; all that we can do is to take the available
facts, and exhibit them in our scientific setting. We cannot any more
than can physics or biology, set forth our scientific facts and uniformities otherwise than in a matrix of logic; all that we can do is to keep the
logic separate from the facts and uniformities, so that on the one hand
the facts are uncoloured by logic and on the other hand the full colour
of the facts appears in our logical conclusions. . . .

—Edward B. Titchener,
Systematic Psychology:
Prolegomena[30]

Select the best title:
   a. "Logical Psychology"
   b. "Is Psychology a Science? Maybe. Maybe Not."
   c. "I Have No Idea What I Am Saying"
   d. "Psychology as a Science"
   e. Other:

3. Threshold limit values refer to airborne concentrations of substances and represent conditions under which it is believed that nearly all workers may be repeatedly exposed day after day without adverse effect. Because of wide variation in individual susceptibility, however, a small percentage of workers may experience discomfort from some substances at concentrations at or below the threshold limit, a smaller percentage may be affected more seriously by aggravation of a preexisting condition or by development of an occupational illness. . . .

> —*"Industrial Ventilation,"* a paper delivered
> at the American Conference of
> Governmental Industrial Hygienists[31]

Select the best title:
   a. "Pollution Makes Some People Sick"
   b. "The Threshold Limit of Pollutants Theory"
   c. "Exposure to Pollution Has Its Limits"
   d. Other:

4. Our story—set in the late 1800s—is about three virginal half-sisters (same mother, different fathers). We open at the reading of Mother's will. Mother was a founding member of Boston's Botanical Bed Society and has named the girls after her favorite flowers: Forsythia, the sweet, frothy young thing; Hardy Mum, the Earth-Mother type; and Pyracantha, a brazen hussy. Pyra is always griping about her name, but her sisters remind her that Mother also loved Spiraea. It seems that Mother was a successful entrepreneur of the boudoir and had been paying off creditors with personal favors. The girls learn they can no longer live in their accustomed style, so they debate whether or not to take up the family business. Unfortunately, none is quite sure about the going rate for personal favors. Enter the family lawyer. Mother has left the girls an estate in southern Illinois, so they take off for the adventurous Midwest. In their travels, they're met by mountain men, a river-boat crew, Indians, river pirates, a traveling preacher named Captain Lee Earl, and his blind sidekick General Quarters. Of course, they're vanquished all along the way. . . .

> —from a rejected trashy novel proposal

Select the best title:
   a.   A Saga of the Old Midwest
   b.   Very Vanquished Virgins
   c.   The Reading of the Will
   d.   Other:

Step 2   Identify Supporting Data within the Passage
   Does the detail within the written passage expand, clarify, illustrate, or restate the main point? Enter the English-class outline and the genesis of memory recall.

The Outline (don't panic—it's just a list)

   Outline the following passage:

Gravity and Centripetal Force
   As the Earth spins through space, we stay on its surface because of two natural phenomena: gravity and centripetal force. These forces, so necessary to our existence, are rarely understood (but, then, even the ignorant won't fall off the planet). Nevertheless, scientists have been able to prove their existence through observations of the attraction of objects to one another. The extent of this attraction depends upon the mass or weight of both objects.
   The most noted student of this principle was Sir Isaac Newton. An apple falls out of a tree and to the ground, Newton theorized, because the Earth has so much mass that it attracts the smaller apple to itself. If an elephant were to fall from that same tree, it would also hit the ground—but with much more force. This is because the gravity needed to attract the elephant is far greater than that needed to attract the apple. If your mind is now leaping to the conclusion that more elephantine weight equals more needed gravity—you've got it. That's what weight really is: the amount of gravity needed to hold something to the planet. (And you've probably held the misconception it had something to do with carbohydrates and fat on your meat.) Without gravity, the apple and the elephant would float into space. No amount of weight would help.
   On a less dense planet or object (such as Mars or the moon), the apple and the elephant would both weigh less. On a more dense planet (like Jupiter), the apple and the elephant would both weigh more. Jupiter is approximately two and one half times more dense than the Earth, therefore the average apple on that planet would weigh

slightly over a pound. The average elephant would weigh fifteen tons. (This may, in fact, be one reason for the scarcity of circuses on Jupiter.)

The mass of the Earth is so great that resultant gravity can keep our moon in its orbit. And the mass of the sun is so great as to keep all of the planets and their assorted attractions in solar orbit.

Objects can escape gravity, however. A helium balloon goes up because helium has such little mass or weight. Helium eventually escapes through pores in the balloon and rises into the layers of gas surrounding the Earth. The empty balloon is once again attracted by gravity and falls to the ground as litter. Think about it. Every time we hold a political convention or open a shopping center, someone, somewhere on the planet, may be pelted with deflated Mickey Mouse heads.

A rocket overcomes gravity by means of another physical principle discussed by Newton: for every action there is an equal and opposite reaction. The rocket blasts a force against the ground that is greater than the force attracting the weight of the rocket to the center of the Earth. The reaction (called *thrust*) sends the rocket skyward until it is away from the Earth's gravitational pull. Upon reentry, the rocket uses reverse thrust to slow the effects of gravity.

To a lesser degree, centripetal force also helps keep us on the Earth. And it is by its very nature a bit more abstract. Like the hormonal content of a birth-control pill, you simply must trust that it's there. When an object rotates around another object, centripetal force is the tendency of the rotating object to move toward the axis (center of the rotation). It's easy to confuse the term with centrifugal force, which is actually just the opposite. Centrifugal force (the resistance of an object to move in a curved path) is why a toddler will sail off a spinning merry-go-round when he releases his grip to wave. It is also the reason why Mr. Wizard never got drenched when swinging that glass of water in an arc over his head.

Possible Outline Format (you may have another)

Keep the outline as simple as possible—use it only to identify topics within the text, and relevant subtopics within each topic. There's no need to replicate those grammar-class outlines full of Roman numerals and a's that cannot exist without b's. You may even reorganize the sequence of events if doing so clarifies meaning.

The Main Idea: Gravity and Centripetal Force
Major Topics:
   • Gravity and centripetal force keep us on the Earth.
   • Gravity is the attraction of objects to one another.
   • Centripetal force is the tendency of a rotating object
     to move toward the axis of rotation.
   • Objects can overcome gravity and centripetal force.
Subtopics:
   • Gravity: dependent upon and relative to weight of
     objects
        Gravity of Earth is strong enough to keep the
     moon in orbit. Gravity of sun keeps all other planets
     in their orbits.
        On Earth, apples require less gravity than ele-
     phants. On a less dense planet, both would weigh
     less and thus require less gravity. On a more dense
     planet, both would weigh more and thus require
     more gravity.
        Gravity was first discussed by Sir Isaac New-
     ton
   • Centripetal force:
     The tendency to move toward axis of rotation.
     Opposite of centrifugal force (resistance of object to
     move in a curved path).
   • Objects can overcome both gravity and centripetal
     force subtopics:
        Helium with less mass than air is one common
     example.
        Rockets are another example in that they exert
     a force greater than gravity. Equal and opposite re-
     action causes rocket lift-off (thrust). Reverse thrust
     slows effects of gravity as rocket returns.

Step 3   Identify the Relationship of Ideas
   Much of what we are asked to comprehend in daily life is
itself disorganized and without pattern. But that which is well

constructed will follow one of four game plans: Chronological Cause-and-Effect, Least-to-Most-Important Cause-and-Effect, Reverse-Sequential (most to least important), and Compare-and-Contrast.

Chronological Cause-and-Effect A chain of chronological events leading up to the main point, climax, or culminating event.
Example:

> She turned off the light and slipped into the coolness of the sheets. Every sound was intense within the silence. A crackling in the roof, the ticking clock, a draft moving a window blind—these things demanded her attention with inflated significance. Suddenly she strained to identify another unfamiliar sound. She was instantly alert. Her eyes opened and scanned the darkness. Her breathing stopped. Her head rose in a smooth, subtle movement as her ears strained to receive even the faintest vibration. Somebody was breaking into the house! Maybe an experienced thief—the kind who when appearing on cable talk shows warns the reverent audience members to stay in their beds while he harmlessly practices his trade. Maybe a maniac—hot in the lust for blood. Perhaps the maniac would pounce upon her bed and bite chunks out of her breast before slitting her throat in a final orgasm. "Holy Mary!" She sat up and turned on the lamp, as if the light would make her hearing more acute. She listened again for that sound. It was the air reverberating through her own slightly clogged nasal passages. God. She hated being alone at night.

Least-to-Most-Important Cause-and-Effect This is often used when reporting an event, a procedure, or an analysis. The main point is presented only after a buildup of supporting ideas. Key words are: *as a result, because, therefore, since, consequently,* and *so.*

Example:

Northwest Territorial Bell
555 Juneau Way
Fridge, Alaska 10000

Persons:

This letter comes after repeated (and unresolved) communication with one of your service representatives: Dinga Ling. After four months of such discord, Ms. Ling has suggested I "go straight to Bell."

We have been in our new residence (phone number 555-5555) for six months and are still receiving calls for the Herman ("Buck") Spenser family. Judging from the volume of incoming day and night telephone encounters, the Spensers may have even crossed wires with a toll-free hot line. Most distressing is the relationship I have developed with Mr. Spenser's Aunt Bellma. This dear lady refuses to accept the fact that I am not Buck's wife, Tricksie. Aunt Bellma phones each morning and most evenings with distress calls and grocery orders. I would contact the appropriate social-service agency, but Aunt Bellma refuses to convey her last name, phone number, or address. She says Buck knows all that and if I were any kind of a wife, I'd ask him.

Somewhere along your vast communication network—lo, as you read this very letter—an eighty-three-year-old woman is expecting Tricksie to deliver a pepperoni pizza and a bottle of Gatorade. I will withhold installation of extensions for my children as long as this woman's fate is on the line.

I thought telephone numbers were allowed to languish for a respectful period of time before being pronounced dead and reassigned to a new customer. Obviously this was incorrect information. Our number was both warm and fertile when assigned to our pole.

Please find Buck, help Aunt Bellma, and change our phone number to one with a bit of rigor mortis.

Yours in angry perpetuity,
Buzzed Off

Reverse-Sequential (most to least important) This is often called the journalistic format since most news stories progress from the "lead" or effect, to the cause of the event. The outline of Gravity and Centripetal Force placed the ideas in this sequence. The most important ideas were listed first, followed by ideas of less importance. For example, the fact that gravity depends upon the weight of objects was judged more important than the fact that this theory was first defined by Newton. Much of the difficulty in comprehending scientific or technical material comes from an inability to differentiate between major and minor points that have been placed out of such a sequence.

A recipe also follows the Reverse-Sequential format. The name of the dish is the main point although the steps in preparation follow a chronological order.

Example:

French Bread with Chives
Spread a sliced loaf of French bread with a mixture of 1 stick softened butter, 1/4 cup sour cream, and 1/4 cup minced chives. Bake at 400° F. for 10 to 15 minutes. Serve warm.

Compare-and-Contrast This format is used with issues and ideas representing distinct viewpoints and dimensions. As you read material organized with this pattern, focus on how information is being balanced.

Key words helpful in identifying this game plan are: *but, nevertheless, on the other hand, still,* and *however.*

Example:

Many résumé experts tell you to boldly list your professional objective (usually the job that's open) at the beginning of the chronological résumé. But there are two sides to this issue. Your doing so certainly makes life easier for all of the assistant résumé shufflers who will handle your paper profile before serious consideration by the *real boss*. Yet such a move can relegate you to an inescapable cubbyhole. You may have applied for the professional objective known as Administrative Task Developer, when you are actually more qualified for another, higher-paid position they call the Director of Executive Achievements. A résumé shuffler who's really *with it* can make the connection. Most aren't and don't.

Traditional intelligence tests most easily address the comprehension tasks of literal understanding (simple vocabulary recognition) and inference (reading between the lines). But when you move beyond IQ questions to real-life adult problem-solving situations, you must utilize two additional skills rarely seen on intelligence tests. These skills are known as *analysis* and *judgment*. Analysis is the evaluation of probable relationships resulting from both literal and implied statements and a formulation of several probable conclusions. Judgment is the placing of a value upon the material comprehended; a state of belief or nonbelief. When you hear a TV debate over nuclear disarmament or when you arbitrate a battle between your kids, you can begin analysis and judgment with the same compare-and-contrast or the same cause-and-effect relationships seen on intelligence tests. And so the skills of verbal comprehension are the foundations of more complex problem-solving skills.

Analysis and judgment also require another preliminary skill seen on intelligence tests: deductive reasoning.

Verbal Deductive Reasoning (Logic)

Deductive reasoning is that thinking process in which the mind moves from a general fact to a specific conclusion while eliminating false or inappropriate alternative conclusions. Keep this term in mind, for deductive reasoning is most necessary for survival in the real world.

Most of us fear deductive reasoning because:

- we assume at first glance that the process is more complicated than a series of simple steps; and
- when we do err in an initial step, our conclusion can be *incredibly* wrong. This makes us look like royal fools.

Let's say I own a gas station. You drive in, hand me fifty cents, and say, "Put this much in the tank. Hurry!"

I can deduce that you are a cheapskate, snort, and make some derogatory remark. But you could be driving a company car that can be filled only by use of the company credit card. You've left the card at your office and need just a tiny bit of gas to make it there and back to the station; fifty cents should just about do it. A fifty-cent deviation in your expense report could be covered with no risk of detection; besides, you've already been formally reprimanded for screwing up on this credit-card business, and you have no more chances. You can't call your secretary because the entire staff is at the boss's wedding. You're late. You would have parked the now-empty car and run to the office—but yesterday your left foot was cut off and your crutches don't fit. See what I mean?

Even a relatively simple vocabulary task (such as finding an antonym) can take on a new and more complex dimension when the test writer constructs the question so that it cannot be answered without deductive reasoning. For example:

In the following series, underline the two words that are opposite in their meanings:

    peanut butter   table   apple   chair   milk

Answer

What association can you make among the elements? Obviously all items are nonliving. Obviously they are from different categories/families. Try an association of a physical state: color? form? smell? At random, you could choose "form."

Peanut butter is soft, table is hard. But so is chair. Therefore, hard/soft is not the criterion for judging opposites here.

This could lead you to make a comparison between table and chair. They may seem to have opposite functions, but you can actually do just about anything on a table you would consider doing on a chair.

Peanut butter is a food from a plant. Milk is a food from an animal. That seems to be stretching the definition of opposite a bit. Better keep that one in reserve.

Milk comes from a cow. Peanut butter, table, and chair come from plants. That won't work; too many plastic chairs around.

But chair, table, and peanut butter are all end results in a process. So's milk—but obviously in a different kind of process. At this point you would begin comparing each item (as an end product) to any other item (as if it were the beginning of a process).

A table or chair doesn't progress to another item—only to a part of a set, e.g., room decoration, set for a school play. (If you momentarily forgot about plastic again, and thought table and chair could progress to firewood, that's called "educational bias," "tunnel vision," or "The Mule Mind-set Syndrome.")

Milk, on the other hand, is the beginning item in several processes. (We may be on a roll here!) Marking peanut butter/milk at this point may be correct; or it may be premature.

Better check peanut butter to apple: Apple can also be the beginning item in several food processes.

Back to peanut butter for some more clues regarding its properties. Peanut butter is the end result of smashing peanuts.

If you smash milk you'll probably regret it, but smashing apples will give you apple sauce (even cider, if you work it right).

Thus, *peanut butter* and *apples* are opposites.

(Now—you may contend that smashing milk in a churn leads to butter. I contend that real butter comes from smashing cream, not milk. I wrote the test question, so *my* contention ends up on the computerized answer sheet. This may be the most important thing you ever learn about IQ tests: they *cannot* totally avoid incorporating the education, biases, and, yes, even factual errors/assumptions of test writers.)

Verbal deductive reasoning is usually presented on intelligence tests as verbal series completion, sentence completion, verbal analogies, syllogisms, and complex deductive puzzles.

Verbal Series Completion

Find the word that goes with the series.
1. Lulu   Marvin   Wonder Woman
    a. Linus
    b. Phyllis Schlafly
    c. desk lamp
    d. peanut
    e. ladybug
2. Metamucil   Ex-Lax   Feen-a-Mint
    a. la Bamba
    b. Drāno
    c. Spic and Span
    d. Fletcher's Castoria
    e. Swift & Natural
3. sprocket   lug   crescent
    a. distributor
    b. telephone
    c. half-moon
    d. goldfish
    e. pipe
4. chocolate pie   avocado   peanut butter
    a. celery
    b. carrot sticks
    c. ice cream
    d. wood chips
    e. mushrooms
5. nylon   orlon   rayon
    a. silk
    b. wool
    c. cotton
    d. saffron
    e. Dacron

Answers

Once again we can see the possibility of cultural bias. In attempting to test the logical thinking process, test writers must assume they have chosen words known to all. But if he doesn't recognize the words, even a deductive genius will fail such verbal tests.

1. While some people could be fooled by **b**, **a** is a comic-strip character like the rest of the series. Extra gifted points if you argue that **d**—peanut—is the singular unit of a Charles Schulz cartoon.

2. While others may have varying degrees of success, **d** is the name-brand laxative.

3. **e** is another type of wrench. Wench is something else, but both can lie next to a screwdriver.

4. I can't believe anyone weighing more than fifty pounds would have missed **c** as a food you can't eat when you're on a diet.

5. I thought you deserved a break.

Sentence Completion

Choose the best word or phrase to complete the sentence.

1. My electric typewriter isn't working, so I'll————.
   a. paint the kitchen
   b. take it to the repair shop
   c. stand it in the corner until it behaves
   d. eat it
   e. beat it to death with a hammer
2. There is no situation in life so————as to be devoid of any lesson.
   a. true
   b. worthless
   c. excellent
   d. ambiguous
   e. like spaghetti sauce
3. At the first sign of a laundry stain, I put the garment in the ————.
   a. washer
   b. mop bucket
   c. sunlight

d. rag bag

e. microwave

4. The most effective treatment for premenstrual syndrome is

   _____.

   a. an apple tree and a serpent

   b. progesterone

   c. estrogen

   d. a shot and a beer

   e. monosodium glutamate

5. I never bother to———the bread before making sandwiches.

   a. toast

   b. picket

   c. thaw

   d. eat

   e. sell

Answers

One sad consequence of the mechanical and mathematical aspects of standardized/computerized intelligence testing is the necessity for *one* single, always/most often—well, usually correct—answer. Computer score sheets cannot facilitate the creative answer, be it ever so intelligent. So a brain adept in creative associations, word play, and pun construction becomes a distinct handicap. When the test taker cannot maintain a tight control over his creativity—in other words, when he cannot keep unconventional thoughts from forcing themselves into his consciousness—this simple test section can turn into an intellectual quagmire. I personally have such painful memories of sections like this one that it hurts to tell you some answers are more correct than are others. But if you're intent upon keeping score, the most probable answers are:

1. **b.**

2. **b.**

3. **a.**

4. **c.**

5. **a.**

If I were answering, I would choose the following:

1. **e.** It's the real me.

2. **d.** Amen.

3.   **d.** Life's entirely too short for trauma over stains.
4.   **a.** Think about it.
5.   **c.** Doesn't everybody freeze it when it's fresh?
(You may have selected others.)

Verbal Analogies

As we've discussed, the figural analogy is a staple of all IQ tests. But the verbal analogy is more typical of the kinds of puzzles you will face in day-to-day adult problem solving.

An intensive study conducted at the University of Minnesota categorized the types of verbal analogy questions most commonly used on intelligence tests.[32] They are

Synonyms or similarities
Antonyms or opposites
Same group or class
Parts of a larger group
Transformation from one group into another
Quantity or quality relationship
Functional relationship
Artificial relationships (letter patterns, word combinations—totally abstract)

Examples of each category are as follows:

1.   Synonyms or similarities:
sad is to *unhappy* as *glad* is to ?
a.   Saran Wrap   b.   happy   c.   sullen   d.   melancholy
e.   popular

Answer
   b.

2.   Antonyms or opposites:
cold is to *hot* as *wet* is to ?
a.   damp   b.   cool   c.   warm   d.   dry
e.   moisture

Answer
   d.

3. Same group or class:
dog is to *cat* as *Labor Day* is to ?
a. beer and bratwurst   **b.** mice   **c.** the Fourth of July
d. flag   **e.** holiday

Answer
 c.

4. Parts of a larger group:
clothing is to *hat* as *food* is to ?
a. pizza   **b.** overcoat   **c.** hegira   **d.** trough   **e.** fat

Answer
 a.

5. Transformation from one group into another:
grape is to *wine* as *paper* is to ?
a. drunk   **b.** tree   **c.** manipulate   **d.** book
e. servitude

Answer
 d.

6. Quantity or quality relationship:
terrific is to *awful* as *few* is to ?
a. muckworm   **b.** many   **c.** none   **d.** horrible
e. necessity

Answer
 b.

7. Functional relationship:
key is to *lock* as *electricity* is to ?
a. door   **b.** swerve   **c.** light bulb   **d.** bird
e. who cares?

Answer
 c.

8.   A purely mechanical/artificial relationship: In this type of verbal analogy, the test writer constructs totally abstract relationships such as:

- letter patterns:

boot is to *tool* as *letter* is to ?
a. hypothecary   **b.** cranium   **c.** rattan   **d.** post office
e. snoot

peal is to *deal* as *hope* is to ?
a. prowl   **b.** dope   **c.** mutual   **d.** girl   **e.** table

Answers

   c. (letter pairs in the center of the word) and **b.** (vowel/consonant groupings)

- word constructions:

meatball is to *sidecar* as *stairstep* is to ?
a. zither   **b.** spaghetti   **c.** carpet   **d.** focus   **e.** bail

Answer

   c.

The list could go on for the length of the test writer's imagination. But, of course, as you sit down to a test, nothing in the instructions tells you precisely *which category* of analogy you are to complete. Part of the test, in fact, is to determine your ability to observe, test, and reject various types of analogies. It can get very confusing. A word can function as that which it represents in reality—or it can function as a part of an abstract/artificial concept. As you work the following verbal analogies, remember a few simple rules:

Step 1   Look for the simplest problem.
Step 2   Try alternatives and eliminate deductive "blind alleys."
Step 3   Review often.
Step 4   Keep your mind open to an artificial relationship.

1. *forint* is to *Hungary* as *dollar* is to ?
    a. U.S.
    b. $10
    c. money
    d. George Washington
    e. greenback
2. jonquil is to daffodil as hyacinth is to?
    a. iris
    b. geranium
    c. onion
    d. tulip
    e. narcissus

Answers

1. If you don't recognize the word *forint*, chances are you will look to the counterpart of Hungary—U.S. (a). Forint *could* be a unit (state or territory) of Hungary (as dollar is a unit of money). But in this case, that idea must be ruled out since dollar is also a unit of ten dollars. The answer is **a**. U.S.

2. Analogies such as that in question 2 have been found on every IQ test I've ever seen. And as in the previous question, it exemplifies how education influences your score. Take it a step at a time.

    Begin with one of the more obvious relationships between jonquils and daffodils: they are flowers, yes—but more specifically, they are flower bulbs. As hyacinth is also a bulb, apply the identical relationship to all alternatives.

    a. Iris is not a bulb but a rhizome. That's similar, but different.

    b. Geraniums come from seeds, so they aren't even close.

    c. Onion is a bulb. Could this be the winner? Look to the next choice, (**d**). A tulip is also a bulb. So much for the bulb theory.

    Try another association. Jonquils and daffodils are usually seen in colors of yellow and white. In nature (as opposed to "in plastic"), hyacinths and narcissis usually exist in shades of red, white, and blue. Forget it—irises come in all those same hues. Besides, an association based upon flags in a parade is quite a stretch.

Try another, more primary association: form. Jonquils and daffodils have similar flower formations. And hyacinths and geraniums, unlike most tulips and irises (we can't be bothered this early in the puzzle with those strange Dutch hybrids), both flower in multitrumpeted formations. But then, so does an onion—we just usually eat it before it gets a chance.

Try another relationship. I always get jonquils and daffodils confused; maybe they're members of the same botanical family. If this were true, what other plant is in the same botanical family as the hyacinth? If during an IQ test you were unsure of this specific fact, you would have to guess—or drop your pencil, walk out of the exam, and look for a dictionary. Simply solving the problem intellectually doesn't count. If, however, you were a horticulturist, or if someone once told you that onions and hyacinths are members of the lily family and that daffodils and jonquils are both types of narcissus—then you could have quickly and correctly answered **c**, onion, without having to go through all of this.

Syllogisms

When most of us think of logic, those neat little syllogisms come to mind. They are the deductive couplets or triplets that lead us to deduce or infer a final truth.

I like white wine better than red wine.
I like champagne better than white wine.
Therefore, I like champagne better than red wine.

In this form, the syllogism seems reasonable, *logical*, and worthy of its universal status. However, when distorted by zeal and ignorance, the honorable syllogism can turn into an instrument of confusion, misrepresentation, and false prophecy. As you approach a written presentation or verbal discussion, you must analyze whether or not any syllogism is sensible or silly. The following represent common abuses of logic.

Silly Syllogisms

Honor by association
Dr. Peterson is a wonderful person.
She thinks this new proposal is okay.
Therefore, this new proposal is wonderful.

The false analogy
Only fools wear cowboy boots.
The President wears cowboy boots.
Therefore, the President is a fool.

Businessmen know sound fiscal strategy.
Senator Jackson is a businessman.
Therefore, Senator Jackson should be our next President
so that he may straighten out our fiscal mess with sound
fiscal strategy.

Each of these examples follows a "logical" order. But does
the logic make sense? In real life, we cannot assume that the
President is a fool solely because of a "logical" relationship to a
"silly premise."

Another type of false analogy is the the *non sequitur*.
(Translation: It does not follow.)

I like fried chicken and apple pie.
I am a good American.
Therefore, anyone who doesn't like fried chicken and apple
pie (a) is probably a Communist, or (b) doesn't like me.

A non sequitur can also take this pattern:

I would never want to go to a basketball game.
Therefore, no one else would ever want to go either.

Other common examples of pseudo logic are:

The absolute proof
Absolutely every employee in this company is 100 percent
behind this project—except you.
Nobody on the entire planet thinks this idea has merit.

Answering the wrong question
Question: "Mr. Mayor, what is your goal for placing His-
panics within your administration?
Answer: "I've always liked tacos. "

The hasty generalization
I am from Indiana.
My friends are from Indiana.
My friends and I don't like TV game shows.
Come to think of it, nobody else in Indiana probably likes
TV game shows either.

Overgeneralization
Your only problem is that you don't think you have a
problem.

As you read the previous exercises in reading comprehension, you may have concluded that some silly syllogisms are
amusing. Those of Woody Allen are downright funny. Humor
uses logic in two distinctively irreverent ways: (1) as a distor-
tion of logic; (2) as the logical extension of an illogical premise.
Thus, when you evaluate a silly syllogism, you must judge
whether it is presented as literal truth or as parody—in other
words, was it *meant* to be silly or not? Once again, judgment of
this nature, while an intricate part of everyday problem solving, never ends up on an IQ, achievement, or aptitude test instrument.

Meanwhile, logic and deductive reasoning can be far more
complex than simple syllogisms:

Complex Deductive Puzzles

As you work through the following exercises (and don't
feel you must accomplish that task during one lunch break),
keep the following dicta in mind:

You can do it if it can be done.
Charting what you know helps.
Make an assumption and carry it through to its logical con-
clusion.

Use the process of elimination until the correct answer
   springs forth.
Review often.
Don't expect to hold everything in your memory.
Don't give up.

Problem 1

You are a federal social-service caseworker. Ninety-year-old triplets, Huey, Dewey, and Louie, enter your office asking for government
retirement benefits. In order to qualify for a disability pension, an individual must have both a Certificate of Medical Necessity, signed by
a physician, and an Employment Quarterly Quota Form.

In order to obtain an Employment Quarterly Quota Form, an individual must have a notarized Sick Leave Permission Slip from his or
her most recent employer. One cannot obtain a notarized Sick Leave
Permission Slip without a Certificate of Medical Necessity. Each of the
triplets (although they worked for the same employer, now deceased)
is either:

Eligible for a Disability Pension,
Eligible for a Retirement Rebate, or
Eligible for both a Disability Pension and a Retirement Rebate.

However, no one can be both eligible for a Retirement Rebate *and*
possess an Employment Quarterly Quota Form.

What can you do to help—

Huey: Who has not collected a notarized Sick Leave Permission
Slip?

Dewey: Who has his Employment Quarterly Quota Form?

Louie: Who has never seen a doctor and claims he will leap into
the "depths of hell" before doing so now?

One plan of action: Outline what you know (don't forget the
converse of known declarations), and make up a key system.

Disability Pension = DP
Certificate of Medical Necessity = CMN
Employment Quarterly Quota = EQQ
Sick Leave Permission Slip = SLPS
Retirement Rebate = RR

Fact 1   If DP, then CMN + EQQ
Fact 2   If EQQ, then SLPS
Fact 3   No SLPS unless CMN
             If CMN, then SLPS
Fact 4   Either DP or RR or both
             If not DP, then RR
             If not RR, then DP
Fact 5   Not RR and EQQ
             If RR, then not EQQ

Solving this problem can be made easier if you learn a basic rule in the game of logic:

When if x, then y is true:
You may *not* deduce if not x, then not y.
You may *not* deduce if y, then x.
But you *may* deduce if not y, then not x.

As you progress through the solution, consult the key, outline, and logic rule.

1. Huey does not have his SLPS.

   Therefore (looking at Fact 2, using the logic rule), Huey does not have an EQQ.

   Therefore (looking at Fact 1), Huey does not have a CMN and an EQQ and, therefore, he is not eligible for a DP.

   But—according to Fact 4—Huey·is eligible for an RR.
2. Dewey has his EQQ.

   Therefore (looking at Fact 2), he also has his SLPS.

   Therefore (looking at Fact 3), he has a CMN.

   Therefore (looking at Fact 5), he is not entitled to an RR.

   But—according to Fact 4—he is eligible for a DP.
3. Louie has never seen a doctor, and *you* don't feel like fighting *that* battle today.

   Therefore, since physicians sign CMNs (looking at the logic rule), Louie does not have a CMN.

Therefore (looking at Fact 3), he does not have the signature of his previous employer on a SLPS.

Therefore (looking at Fact 2), he does not have his EQQ.

Therefore (looking at Fact 1), he is not eligible for a DP.

But—according to Fact 4—he is eligible for an RR.

Solution

Huey gets a Retirement Rebate.
Dewey gets a Disability Pension.
Louie gets a Retirement Rebate.

And who says social-service caseworkers sit on their duffs all day while the rest of us work for the money they hand out? The caseworker probably also had to see that the guys got a ride home.

Problem 2

You are employed by a small but prosperous family business. It's your first day on the job—and it's been a disaster! First, your boss called in sick. Now, at 5:05 P.M., everyone has fled the building. You discover a note telling you the three chief officers and their spouses are having an anniversary celebration in the company dining room. You are to distribute the name cards. Your boss has left the cards, a set of instructions, and directions to the dining room (nobody ever bothered to give you a tour). The names printed on the cards are: Benji, Chuck, Junior, Elaine, Sissy, and Bernice. You have no idea who any of these people are. But the company is called Peterson, Armstrong, Peterson, and Branif. The boss's instructions are:

Place the cards in male/female/male order around the table. *Do not* place anyone next to his or her own spouse. Elaine and Mrs. Peterson like to smoke, as do the president's spouse and Mr. Branif; put the crystal ashtrays at their places. The treasurer (did you know she was an only child?) wants Benji to sit on her right. The chairman of the board wants to sit nearer to Chuck than to Mr. Armstrong. Sissy is the president's sister-in-law and her only brother is on her left. (That's Sissy's only brother, because the president is also an only child.) Have fun.

You've tried calling the boss—no answer. You have a final exam at night school, so you can't stay to meet the officers, and ask for help. All the secretaries have locked their desks and file cabinets, so you can't even find a company letterhead for more clues. (Naturally, the boss didn't leave any in your desk and the note is written on plain paper.) You open the phone book, but can make no connection in the residential listings between the three known surnames and the names on the place cards. You call the public library, but the reference librarian (who could have looked the company up in *Dun & Bradstreet*) has gone for the day. The night watchman seems to be on Quaaludes and is absolutely no help. The County Clerk's office is closed, so you can't look up the papers of incorporation. Where do you place those damn cards (and still keep your job)?

One plan of action:
Begin by outlining the facts.

> **Fact 1** Elaine, Mrs. Peterson, the president's spouse, and Mr. Branif smoke.
> **Fact 2** The treasurer (she's an only child) wants Benji sitting on her right.
> **Fact 3** The chairman of the board is to sit nearer to Chuck than to Mr. Armstrong.
> **Fact 4** Sissy is the president's sister-in-law. Sissy's only brother, the president's spouse, is sitting on her left.
> **Fact 5** The president has no brother.
> **Fact 6** Place cards in male/female order.

You learn from Fact 2 that the treasurer is a female.
You learn from Fact 4 that Sissy:

• Is not the president.
• Has a brother.

Returning to Fact 2, Sissy cannot be the treasurer since she is not an only child. We also know from Fact 3 that the chairman of the board is a woman—remember our male/female order. If the COB were a male—

Male COB

—Chuck and Mr. Armstrong would be of equal distance from him. But when the COB is female:

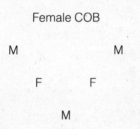

Female COB

you can seat one male (namely, Mr. Armstrong) farther away than the other two.

Since Sissy cannot be the treasurer, nor the president, nor the president's sister-in-law, we also know that only she can be the chairman of the board. Go to the table and give Sissy any chair.

Sissy
Chairman of Board

A   B

C   D

E

Returning to Fact 3, Sissy must sit next to Chuck—and all parties must be seated in male/female/male order. Thus Chuck must be in either Seat A or Seat B. Also, the males sitting in Seats A and B must not be her husband. Only one seat remains for a male (Seat E). Therefore, Sissy Armstrong must be seated *across* from her husband, Mr. Armstrong (Seat E).

Sissy Armstrong
Chairman of the Board

Seat A   Seat B

Seat C   Seat D

Mr. Armstrong

Fact 4 tells you that Sissy's brother, the president's spouse, must be seated on Sissy's left. Therefore, the president's husband is to be seated in Seat B. Since the president can't sit next to her husband, the only female seat for the president is Seat C. Chuck, per the COB's request, is in Seat A.

Sissy Armstrong
Chairman of the Board

Chuck   Husband of
                                                President

President   Seat D

Mr. Armstrong

Fact 1 tells you that the president's spouse is *not* Mr. Branif. Therefore, the president and her husband are Mr. and Mrs. Peterson. Also, since Mrs. Peterson is neither Sissy nor Elaine, her name must be Bernice.

Sissy Armstrong
Chairman of the Board

Chuck   Mr. Peterson

Bernice Peterson   Seat D
President
Mr. Armstrong

The complete solution is close at hand. Obviously Seat D is to be occupied by a female who is also the treasurer of the company. Therefore: Mr. Peterson (sitting to the right of the treasurer) is Benji; the treasurer's first name is Elaine; she and her husband are the Branifs, and Mr. Armstrong is Junior.

Sissy Armstrong
Chairman of the Board

Chuck Branif   Benji Peterson

Bernice Peterson   Elaine Branif
President   Treasurer

Junior Armstrong

If you find yourself mentally screaming: "Who *says* the treasurer is a female only child?" then you are too smart for the test. You are thinking beyond the bounds of the game.

(By the way, if I were you, I'd start looking for another job. Your boss is a sadist.)

Problem 3

This year your garden has yielded a bumper crop of carrots, beets, tomatoes, and zucchini. You've canned dozens of quarts of unseasoned vegetables, and now you'd like to try something different. In an old Shaker cookbook you find recipes for canned vegetables that are pickled, spiced, peppered, or candied. But, although you would love to experiment, four different processes can be very time-consuming. You decide to season 1 quart of each vegetable with a different recipe, and you want to process (cook) all 4 quarts at once. So you need to decide which vegetable is to be pickled, which spiced, which peppered, and which candied. Each vegetable must cook a specific amount of time, and each time is different—but you can still devise a plan.

As you sit down to prepare your cooking schedule, you already know the following facts:

> *Fact 1* In the pressure cooker, beets must be placed next to the peppered vegetable. The peppered vegetable came from the northern part of the garden.
>
> *Fact 2* The quart of tomatoes must boil 40 minutes.
>
> *Fact 3* The quart of spiced vegetables must boil 3 minutes less than the pickled.
>
> *Fact 4* The carrots boil 35 minutes.
>
> *Fact 5* The zucchini, which cooks 1 minute less than the beets, was grown in the southern part of the garden. You also decide that you want to preserve the zucchini with its peel, and the thought of spiced zucchini peel turns your stomach.

Fact 6 The peppered vegetable must cook more than 5 minutes longer than the candied vegetable.

How do you prepare each vegetable, and how long does each quart boil in the pot?

One plan of action for solving this type of complex deductive-reasoning problem is to use a diagram or grid. Chart known information and proceed to *eliminate* false choices (mark them with an X).

	Pickled	Spiced	Peppered	Candied	Time
Carrots					
Beets					
Tomatoes					
Zucchini					

First, chart what you know: Beets are next to the peppered vegetable, so beets are not peppered. Tomatoes boil 40 minutes, and carrots boil 35 minutes. Zucchini was grown in the southern part of the garden, and the peppered vegetable was grown in the northern part of the garden, so zucchini is not peppered.

	Pickled	Spiced	Peppered	Candied	Time
Carrots					35 min.
Beets			X		
Tomatoes					40 min.
Zucchini		X	X		

As you proceed to analyze and eliminate other factors, include them in your diagram:

If carrots (cooking 35 minutes) were candied, then tomatoes (cooking 40 minutes) would be peppered. But the time difference is exactly 5 minutes and Fact 6 stated that the peppered vegetable must cook *more* than 5 minutes longer than the candied vegetable. Therefore, the carrots will not be candied. Too bad; candied carrots are delicious. Place an X under candied carrots.

If the tomatoes (cooking 40 minutes) were candied, then the only vegetable that could be peppered would be the 35-minute carrots. But we know the peppered vegetable must cook more than 5 minutes longer than the candied; therefore, tomatoes cannot be candied. Add another X.

If the tomatoes (cooking 40 minutes) were spiced, then the process of elimination would tell you that carrots (cooking 35 minutes) must be peppered—and beets and zucchini must be either pickled or candied. But the pickled vegetable would then be cooked 43 minutes (review Fact 3), and the peppered vegetable is to be cooked more than 5 minutes longer than the candied (Fact 6). But Fact 5 tells us that zucchini and beets differ only by 1 minute's cooking time. Therefore, tomatoes are not to be spiced (add an X).

At this point, relax, have a drink, and review the bidding. Your diagram should look like this:

	Pickled	Spiced	Peppered	Candied	Time
Carrots				X	35 min.
Beets			X		
Tomatoes		X		X	40 min.
Zucchini		X	X		

Make another assumption and run it through the same process:

If carrots (cooking 35 minutes) were to be peppered, then by elimination tomatoes (cooking 40 minutes) would be pickled, while beets and zucchini would be either spiced or candied.

If that were true, then the spiced vegetable would be cooked 37 minutes (review Fact 3), and the candied vegetable would be cooked less than 30 minutes (review Fact 6). Also, in this case, the peppered vegetable would be cooked for 35 minutes. *But*—beets and zucchini differ by only 1 minute in their cooking times (damn that Fact 5). However, you may take heart in the knowledge that all this has proven that carrots cannot be peppered. Thank God.

By the process of elimination, we have learned our first bit of really good news. We know—without doubt—that the tomatoes are to be peppered! Place a star or two on your diagram. And while you're at it, rule out pickled tomatoes as well.

If the carrots (cooking 35 minutes) were to be spiced, then they would also cook longer than the candied vegetable because (reviewing Fact 6) the peppered tomatoes are cooked 40 minutes, which should be 5 minutes longer than the candied. Also, the pickled vegetable (which, as everybody knows from Fact 3, is to be cooked 3 minutes more than the spiced) would then have to be cooked 38 minutes. *But*—beets and zucchini would have to be pickled or candied—and good ol' Fact 5 reminds us that their cooking times would then exceed the 1-minute interval. Therefore, the carrots could not be spiced.

Time to review:

	Pickled	Spiced	Peppered	Candied	Time
Carrots		?	X	X	35 min.
Beets		X			
Tomatoes	X	X	*	X	40 min.
Zucchini		X	X		

Peppered are cooked "more than 5 minutes" longer than candied (Fact 6).

Beets are cooked 1 minute more than zucchini (Fact 5).

Pickled are cooked 3 minutes more than spiced (Fact 3).

Therefore: If peppered were cooked 40 minutes, then candied must be cooked "more than 5 minutes" less than 40 (Fact 6). If carrots (35 minutes) were spiced, then pickled must be 38 (Fact 3).

Therefore: Pickled could only be beets or zucchini (they are 1 minute apart).

Therefore: If beets were pickled and cooked 38 minutes,

then zucchini would have to be candied and cooked 37 minutes (Fact 5).

But—37 minutes is not "more than 5 minutes less" than 40 minutes (peppered).

Therefore: In the spiced-carrots scenario, zucchini could not be candied. Conversely, if zucchini were pickled and cooked 38 minutes, then beets would be candied and cooked 35 minutes. (And 35 is definitely *not* 1 more than 38.)

Therefore: By the process of elimination, we now know that carrots cannot be spiced.

Look once again to the chart.

	Pickled	Spiced	Peppered	Candied	Time
Carrots		X	X	X	35 min.
Beets			X	X	
Tomatoes	X	X	*	X	40 min.
Zucchini		X	X		

Since we've eliminated the spiced carrots, only beets remain. Beets are to be spiced; add a star, and put an X under pickled and candied.

	Pickled	Spiced	Peppered	Candied	Time
Carrots		X	X	X	35 min.
Beets	X	*	X	X	
Tomatoes	X	X	*	X	40 min.
Zucchini		X	X		

Zucchini is the only remaining vegetable that can be candied (peel and all). Add a star to the appropriate spot on the chart, and an X to the pickled-zucchini spot. The only vegetable that can be pickled is carrots. (Of course, you spotted that a few steps ago.)

Carrots are to be pickled and cooked for 35 minutes.

Beets are to be spiced and cooked for 32 minutes.

Tomatoes are to be peppered and cooked for 40 minutes. (My mother says they'll be overdone.)

Zucchini is to be candied and cooked for 31 minutes.

All of which proves precisely why so many people frequent the deli.

Now that you've been initiated, try your hand at some more deductive puzzles:

1. Jason, Bart, Chad, Sluggo, and Matt are all members of Phi Lambda Oopsalon. The five of them have a runoff to see who will represent the fraternity in the Tri-State University intramural games. Matt did not come in first. Chad was two places behind Sluggo, who was not second. Jason was neither first nor last. Bart was one place behind Matt.

In what order did the guys complete the race? (There were no ties.)

2. You go to the Teasdale family reunion and find yourself in a circle with Kathy, Ralph, Karl, Sarah, and Dave. All are related to one another. Four of them try introducing you to one of the others. Each makes one of the following statements:

Statement A "Karl is my son-in-law's brother."
Statement B "Sarah is my mother-in-law."
Statement C "Kathy is my brother's wife."
Statement D "Ralph is my father's brother."

Each person mentioned is one of the five. Who made which statement and how are the five people related?

3. The president is considering four individuals as vice-presidential running mates in the upcoming election. They are: Barbara Jackson, Jane Dole, Elizabeth Jordan, and Jessie Fonda. Three presidential aides (Fuller, Peterson, and Emge) ponder the possibilities.

Fuller thinks it will be either Barbara Jackson or Jane Dole. Peterson is certain it will not be Barbara Jackson. And Emge believes that neither Jane Dole nor Jessie Fonda stands a chance. Only one aide will be correct.

Which running mate will the president select?

Answers

1. Sluggo, Jason, Chad, Matt, and Bart.
2. Statement A was made by Sarah; B was made by Ralph; C was made by Karl; D was made by Dave.

Ralph and Karl are brothers. Sarah is Kathy's mother. Dave is Karl's son.

3. The president will select Jessie Fonda.

It's important to restate the limitations of this kind of puzzle solving. Learning to unravel complex puzzles in deductive reasoning can help you tackle *real-life* problems, but such skill is by no means a panacea. Logic is not necessarily truth. Remember the rule of logic discussed in the Huey, Dewey, and Louie exercise?

> When if x, then y is true:
> You may *not* deduce if not x, then not y.
> You may *not* deduce if y, then x.
> But you *may* deduce if not y, then not x.

Let's translate.

> *When if x, then y is true*
> If you are a girl, then you are also a cheerleader.

> *You may not deduce if not x, then not y*
> But it is not necessarily true that if you are not a girl, you are not a cheerleader (boys do it all the time).

> *You may not deduce if y, then x*
> Conversely, it is not necessarily true that if you are a cheerleader then you must also be a girl.

> *But you* may *deduce if not y, then not x*
> Therefore, if you are not a cheerleader, then you are not a girl. (I seem to remember arguing against that kind of logic for most of my life.)

Such an intellectual blind alley clearly illustrates how the "game of logic" conflicts with real-life problem solving. First, life is rarely as pat as a puzzle. In a *game* the "if x" statement must be so restrictive as to read: "if absolutely, inclusively, positively, for all times x—then y; or *all* girls are also cheerleaders."

Then, too, in real-life problem solving, you are rarely privy to insights as meaningful as: "Beets are cooked 1 minute longer than zucchini" or "The peppered vegetable grew on the northern side of the garden." You may detour into a dozen blind alleys before finding the appropriate spot for a neat little syllogism.

Finally, as you face real-life problems, those step-by-step proddings that prove so successful in deductive-reasoning puzzles or test items can actually become your downfall. As you obey the rules of a puzzle, you can fail to leap beyond the *probable* solution to a much more imaginative and ultimately correct one. Most puzzles have only one correct answer, while most real-life problems can have several. Ultimately, then, it is tenacity, intuition, motivation, confidence, and all those other *nonmeasurable* elements of intelligence that separate the puzzle players from the problem solvers.

Examples of the Real-Life Problem-Solving Process
Our first example was illustrated in the PBS television series, "This Old House." You are covering a ratty old floor with new 9-foot pine planks. You nail the first plank to the floor and merrily begin securing the second. But pine is a soft wood, and such planks often season with a slight bend. The second plank is crooked and won't cooperate as you try abutting it to the first. At the end of the flooring you end up with a seam like this, where the right-hand plank is secured to the floor:

You must push the second plank to the first with even pressure so as not to mar or crack either. What can you do?

Solution

Using deductive reasoning and a figural analogy: Construct two hardwood triangular wedges, each slightly larger than the triangular gap between the planks. Secure the first wedge (shown to the upper left of the two planks) several inches from the second plank. Be certain that the wedge is placed on the same axis as the space between the two planks.

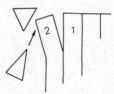

Drive the second wedge into the triangular space between the first wedge and the second plank until both planks abut.

Secure the second plank to the floor. Remove the wedges.

The solution to such a problem seems simple now—but a *very* clever person first devised this scheme. And I can assure you the accomplishment never merited credit on an intelligence test.

In our next example, you have come across an unfamiliar term—out of context—and you can't find it in the dictionary. The word is *diegohrenia*. How can you deduce the definition?

One plan of action: First, find a crossword-puzzle whiz and ask. If he or she doesn't recognize the word, you might begin with a reference text of foreign extractions. (Most English words are composed of root words from other languages.)

Your odyssey could progress like this:

Diego happens to be Spanish for "James."

Die happens to be German for "the."

Speaking of things German: you spot the *ego* and remember that Freud was Austrian (which is close enough). Maybe the word has something to do with Freudian theory.

Diego—James, the Spanish ego.

Can't be.

But *Di* is Latin for "two" or "double." Hello. Freud was always talking about an ego split in two.

Now to *hrenia*.

Nothing can be found in the foreign-extraction dictionary, so you should look for a simpler problem. *Hr* is a very extraordinary diphthong in English. (Enter the skills of long-term memory and lots of experience.) Why not try an assumption H is an error? (Enter the skill of risk taking.) Try applying other letters to the suffix *-renia*. (Enter good ol' tenacity and "perspiratory genius.")

Arenia—sounds better than it really is. No such word.

Brenia—could be an ethnic side dish.

Crenia—isn't he an actor?

Drenia and *erenia*—both sound like something you'd pick up at summer camp.

Frenia. From somewhere in your distant past you remember something called a *frenum*. And you think you recall overhearing in sophomore Latin that the plural of *-um* was either *-a*, *-ae*, or *-ia*. Frenum turns out to be that little flap of skin holding your tongue to the floor of your mouth. Not even Freud was *that* strange.

Forget the possibility that *h* may be a mistake and move on.

Renia. *Reni* means "pertaining to the kidneys." (Two egos and a kidney? That can't be right.) Return to the simplest problem.

Prodding through the alphabet, you eventually come upon *prenia*. Once again the memory banks come through: *p* + *hrenia* = *phrenia*—Latin for "of the mind."

Di + *ego* + *phrenia*. Some fool left out the *p*.

Therefore, your corrected word could mean "of James's mind," but it probably doesn't.

Diegophrenia: a state of mind in which the ego is double or split. A perfectly plausible psychological buzz word. If you still feel ambivalent, you can call a psychoanalyst to cross-check your conclusion.

The key to solving such problems is in the development of skills far more complex and commonplace than those addressed by tests. I'm talking about the adult skills of analysis, judgment, evaluation, and creativity. In the following chapters, you can evaluate your proficiency in those higher levels of learning, intelligence, and accomplishment that are *not* measured by either the IQ or the SAT.

3

Adult Intelligence

Beyond IQ

To this point I've asked you to examine your previous assumptions regarding the *official* measurements of intelligence—to recognize their limitations and flaws. I've asked you to question whether or not you have been evaluating your own intelligence and potential for intellectual growth with these limited tools. In doing so, I'm also asking you to accept what may be for you a new, more expansive, more elusive definition of intelligence. I'm asking you to step beyond the security of a nice, neat little IQ number—beyond the comfort of your past educational status—and think about how smart you really could become.

To do this we must now discuss adult intelligence with reference to three crucial questions:

What is it?
How did you get it?
How can you get more?

WHAT IS IT?

If IQ is an attempt to define six to eight basic, childlike thinking skills—what other, more complex elements comprise adult intelligence?

This question was catapulted beyond rhetoric when World War II forced military analysts once again to decide which man should have which battle placement. One psychologist assigned to this role with the U.S. Navy was Dr. J. P. Guilford. The responsibility of wartime deployment weighed heavily on Guilford as he tried to formulate an evaluation of intelligence that would be more accurate and more inclusive than the old IQ. The products of his search led to a totally new theory of adult human intelligence: the Structure of the Intellect (SOI) model.[1]

A New Look at the Vastness of Intelligence

After the war, Dr. Guilford set about convincing his peers that intelligence is far more complex than ever indicated by the six to eight mental functions represented on either the IQ test or the multiple-aptitude battery. He theorized that the various combinations of these functions and their more abstract applications such as synthesis, analysis, and judgmental skills could be organized into as many as 120 separate mental functions.

Guilford also argued that even abstract reasoning could be taught.[2] This concept is significant as we look to a new definition of intelligence because one premise of IQ and aptitude tests is that abstract reasoning ability is the core of that old representation of intelligence as a static, innate, and therefore measurable commodity. If the very commodity the test attempts to measure is changeable and influenced by learning, then the entire viewpoint of the exercise takes a radical turn. IQ and aptitude tests become gauges of progress—not statements of ability.

But perhaps Guilford's major contribution to gifted education was his contention that creativity and the affective skills of human interaction are as much a part of the intellect as are abstract reasoning skills. Remember, creativity has always been a liability when taking an IQ/aptitude test. And although an attempt was made in early IQ tests, human interaction (or social skills) has not been successfully integrated into standardized testing mechanisms. Both creativity and social skills have always presented monumental problems of interpretation, evaluation, removal of bias, and so forth when applied to any mass statistical formula or scale.

This fundamentally new idea led to the conclusion that creativity may be either synonymous with abstract reasoning *or*, in fact, *the most complex manifestation of abstract reasoning.*[3]

Guilford's theory perceived intelligence in three dimensions:

1. *Contents*—incoming stimuli causing us to use intelligence; material for thought.
2. *Operations*—the functions of intelligence that constitute our behavior as we "react intelligently."
3. *Products*—the organizational patterns that result from thinking; these are the end results of intelligence.

Each intellectual task or entity, then, must be recognized in terms of the kind of material being processed, the type or kind of intellectual process employed, and the resulting product: thought.

Guilford broke down each of his three dimensions into subgroups.[4]

Contents

Figural. These are the concrete objects and forms we perceive visually—cubes, landscapes, and objects—as well as conceptualizations gathered by all our other senses.

Symbolic. These are the codes—tokens such as letters and numbers—we establish for communication with others, as well as for *mental notations* to ourselves.

Semantic. These are thoughts expressed as preassigned or identified words—words, of course, that conjure up abstract meanings.

Behavioral. Still largely unexplored, this category represents those often nonverbal human actions that Guilford called "mental states."

Operations

Cognition. Also called *comprehension* or *understanding*, this is awareness or recognition of data.

Memory. The retention or storage of data with a degree of availability.

Convergent Production. Convergence upon the single, conventionally correct answer (as illustrated by IQ and aptitude test questions).

Divergent Production. Acceptance of many equally valid answers; usually thought of as creativity.

Evaluation. This entails using the previous four processes to analyze data and come to some judgment or independent conclusion for a specific set of circumstances.

Products

Units. These are one figure, one symbol, and so forth.

Classes. Sets or groups of like units.

Relations. The interactions between classes and units. Almost all IQ test questions ask you to identify this particular product of intelligence. A code is the relationship between symbols, just as vocabulary is a semantic relationship between a word and its meaning.

Systems. These constitute a more complex relations pattern: the big picture of interrelated or interacting parts. The sociological precursors to a war illustrate such a pattern.

Transformations. A more abstract ability, transformation requires redefinitions and modifications of existing data. One example would be how the ending of a story is changed to present a new interpretation of the original theme.

Implications. The most abstract category, implication involves the anticipation and/or extrapolation of consequences.

The key to Guilford's concept is that any given intellectual expression (thought) is composed of multiple combinations of these elements. The 120 intellectual tasks Guilford initially identified were permutations of 4 Contents x 5 Operations x 6 Products = 120. For example, identifying a number series on an IQ test would consist of a Symbolic Cognition or Convergence of a Relationship. The creation of a pun would be use of Divergent Production to result in a Semantic Transformation.

It was by analyzing intelligence in this way that Guilford began formally to address and give credence to numerous intellectual tasks that had never been tested in the traditional manner. One such test-neglected skill is the cognition necessary when you process cues in the observable behavior of others (human-relations skills). You see a man who appears to be angry, but you decide he is actually concerned. In this situation, Guilford says you are cognitively processing a behavioral cue (Evaluation) into a Transformation (one of his products of intelligence.) This transformation is possible because of previous knowledge and memory of societal relationships between facial expression, body posture, tone of voice, emotion, and so on.

But Guilford was a good and scholarly psychologist, and so he wanted such skills to be measurable and verifiable and believable to other scholars. To achieve this end, he proposed to measure human-relations skills with test items such as the following.[5]

Imagine the head in the top row as it would appear on the body. Decide which of the three heads in the bottom row would represent the greatest transformation of emotion.

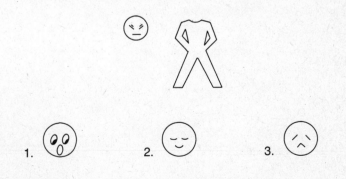

1.   2.   3.

Once again we see the problems inherent in the standard-
ization of test responses. Even as it reaches for more complex
human-relations abilities, such a test must still be limited to a
primary element of the skill.

Our abilities to learn such primary elements of human-
relations skills apparently begin very early. Tests involving infants (average age, thirty-six hours) revealed that the babies
could discriminate between three facial expressions (happy,
sad, and surprised) when presented with a model who inter-
mittently changed moods. Observers registered diminished
visual fixation on one expression and renewed fixation on a second expression as the indication of when, and to what extent,
the babies could notice the change. Furthermore, while the observers were unable to see the model, they were able to guess
at a greater-than-chance accuracy which mood was being displayed. This was possible because of frequent facial mimicking
of the infants.[6]

A major portion of your everyday problem-solving experiences involves the use of more complex human-relations
skills:

"I get the impression something's troubling you today."
"What did she really mean when she said that?"
"You think that was a dumb idea, right?"
"Was that guy telling me the truth about this thing?"

But human-relations skills are most necessary when your
final step in a complex action (such as problem solving) is dependent upon your ability to motivate others.

The most apparent human-relations skills are:

Listening
Successfully communicating
Caring
Identifying needs and wants of others
Melding your needs and wants with those you observe in
    others
Negotiating
Compromising

None of these skills are present on any aptitude, IQ, or achievement test you've ever taken. The very complexity of the exercise and its interpretation prohibits its inclusion on any mathematically standardized test. Moreover, unless you are fortunate enough to have held a supervisory, managerial, or trained voluntary position within a progressive company or organization, little of your formal education has ever focused upon refining this vast area of your intellectual ability. (The one exception, of course, would be professional mental caretakers such as counselors, nurses, and therapists.)

Meanwhile, if you have accelerated yourself to genius-level activities in the area of human relations, your only indication of such an accomplishment may be when others:

Elect you as leader or representative of the group
Invite you to all the parties
Ask your opinion in matters of great importance to them
Say you have a *terrific personality*
Listen when you have something to say
Come to you with all of their personal problems

The complexity of this kind of cognitive achievement is enormous. It is also *learned.* Interpretation of the theories of Guilford is the basis for much of what we see as gifted education in our schools today. It's also a basic element in the human-relations/staff-development philosophies currently practiced within business and industry. SOI theories have gained such momentum in the practical arenas of learning that it's hard to imagine a teacher in this society who doesn't acknowledge divergent thinking or a personnel director who doesn't spend time consulting middle managers on ways to motivate workers.

How Did You Get It? or How Much Genius Is Genetic?

Only a fool would ignore the influence of heredity upon all behavior, including intelligence. The physical influences of genetics can be seen in everything from Mendel's peas to Kentucky's racehorses. For humans, this is nowhere more apparent than in the areas of athletic ability and musical talent. I *could learn* to be an incredibly intelligent football player. But my genetically determined physique cannot compete against most individuals who have passed puberty. I *could learn* to sing with creative brilliance. But my genetically determined vocal folds and facial resonating chambers mean I'll never sound like Barbra Streisand (not even close!).

Nevertheless, many scientists are coming to the conclusion that genetics plays only the most preliminary role in shaping the complex final product of intelligence. Biological anthropologist Dr. Melvin Konner states, "in the real world, the nongenetic sources of variation in behavior may be so large as to swamp any effects of the genes. This does not mean that the genetic change is not occurring or is without effect. It just means that it is slow and small compared to other forces, and that it will therefore be unhelpful to us in our effort to explain what we see and predict what will happen next. . . ."[7]

At this very moment, neuroscientists are trying to decode the genetically electrochemical properties of intelligence. If they ever find the key, you can volunteer to take the smart pill. Others are exploring the genetic folds and convolutions of the brain's surface for a physical map of intelligence. If they ever find that—you can stand in line for a "neuroplasty" (a brain lift). But for now you needn't bother with the theoretical and esoteric arguments about the relative value of genetics to genius or wait for future scientific shortcuts to smartness. We already have astonishing evidence that the physical act of learning actually changes the very nature and structure of your brain cells.

Improving upon Nature
(A brief sojourn into Biology 101)

Conducting learning experiments with human brains and then extracting tangible physical evidence of brain alteration has always presented enormous problems. In the first place, the brain you wish to study may have entirely different views on the matter. Historically, scientists and physicians were forced to study the physical characteristics of functioning human brains exposed by trauma. The only alternative was the clinical exploration of rat, cat, and monkey brains. But recent technology has produced Positron Emission Transaxial Tomography or PETT scan, in which radioactive isotopes within the functioning human brain become visible through the use of computer graphics. We can thus observe physical changes when an individual concentrates upon a specific concept, solves a problem, uses long-term memory, or creates.

With knowledge gained from the rat brains and the PETT scans, the total picture is beginning to come into focus. Thinking (the physical process of intelligence) occurs when an electrical impulse travels up a neurological pathway called the *axon* (or transmitter) and leaps across a void that is at once both infinitesimal and mammoth to another neurological pathway, the *dendrite* (or receiver). This leaping, sparklike action is called the *synapse*. Chemicals and hormones line the pathways, sometimes facilitating the electrical spark and sometimes impeding it. Billions of these synaptic transmissions are snapping back and forth, amid the chemicals and hormones, every moment of your life.[8] Thinking is truly an exciting and kinetic event!

Meanwhile, we know that dendrites (receivers) are lined with spines or points of reception. The greater the number of spines, the greater the number of chances for reception, and, perhaps, the more intense and advanced the process of thinking.[9]

It seems that the electrical impact upon one of these spines causes its usually long, slender shape to compress into a short, stubby one. This state, lasting only a few minutes, would be what we often observe as true *short-term* memory. After this initial impact the transmission is moved on for higher processing, stored as long-term memory at another brain site, or dissipated and forgotten.[10]

Currently there are cavernous gaps in our understanding. For example, postmortem examinations of genetically abnormal and neurologically dysfunctioning brains have revealed dendritic areas totally devoid of spines. How did this happen? Can it be halted? Can it be reversed? Library rooms are filled with documentation and cross-documentation of this odyssey toward biological truth. For our purposes—the question of whether or not learning can physically alter the brain—I will cite only one study. But it's a rather spectacular one.

In an often replicated experiment (first conducted at the University of California, Berkeley), rats were placed in a learning environment: daily exercises, toys, puzzles and lessons, a variety of foods and physical stimuli, as well as contact with other rats and humans. At the same time their genetically identical siblings were kept in a totally deprived environment. Brain tissues from both groups were then analyzed. The *enriched* rats had grown more neurological spines as a direct result of learning.[11] I feel uneasy about summing up the professional crescendos of so many scientists in a simple paragraph, but to repeat the bottom line: *learning can physically increase neurological receptors.* Learning can increase your ability and potential to learn more.

And, God love those scientists, they tried the same experiment with *old* rats. Elderly rats, given an opportunity to participate in (not just watch) the enriched environment, also displayed significant increases in dendritic spines.[12] Old rats got smarter when given new tricks!

IQ and aptitude tests are based upon the assumption that you have a fixed and measurable intellectual capacity: a pot to be filled. But these studies prove that the filling process itself can make your genetically determined container more complex (we could even say *bigger*) than it was when you were born. It matters little then what genetic pattern you began with if learning can physically change it.

There is a traditional concept—now challenged—that specific intellectual processes are conducted in specific brain sites (the Theory of Hemispherical Dominance will be discussed again in chapter 4). But as far back as 1844, Dr. A. L. Wigan published an account of an illness, death, and startling postmortem that was to shake this assumption. Dr. Wigan's patient, although appearing normal in all mental functions, possessed only one cerebral hemisphere—half of a brain, half of his "functioning" brain sites, and presumably an abnormally low number of dendrites. More recently, PETT scans of individuals with severe brain damage and/or pathology have found others who have so compensated for enormous physical loss that remaining portions of the brain seem to have "taken over" for certain functions of intelligence traditionally attributed to the damaged site. An English physician reexamining adults once diagnosed as having childhood hydrocephalis (an accumulation of brain fluids, which, if untreated, results in extensive brain destruction and resultant retardation) found that four individuals had fully recovered and were, in fact, leading normal, productive lives. All had obtained advanced academic degrees and one had even been proclaimed a mathematical genius. Isotopic probes of the electrochemical activity within each patient's brain revealed significant cerebral areas *totally void* of functioning tissue. In the most remarkable case, the only functioning brain tissue appeared to be located within the medulla oblongata (an area situated at the base of the brain and historically credited with control of involuntary functions such as breathing, circulation, and swallowing). Surely a brain capable of rerouting stimuli around malfunctioning or missing tissue would be the Golden Fleece of every educational Argonaut since Socrates.

How can these physical changes be encouraged? That is the core of this section's final question:

How Can You Get More?

Intelligence—even genius—is learned. Understanding this learning process can be of tremendous benefit to you. First, it can help you identify and compensate for prior educational weaknesses. More important, it can help you recognize intellectual potentials you've already accomplished.

General Facts about Learning

Learning causes physical changes in brain cells.
You probably prefer to learn through a dominant sense—
    but you learn most when you involve several senses.
You learn if you want to.

You learn if you have to.

You learn when you receive or create opportunities.

You learn if you refine your skills of observation (memory input).

You learn if you associate a new item with an already learned item.

You learn if you receive intermittent reinforcement (be it reward or punishment).

You are dulled by constant reinforcement—that's why nagging somebody rarely works.

You learn when you enact or practice.

We have the educational technology necessary to greatly increase intelligence display and rates of learning, so if you haven't got it yet—you can still get it. Here's how.

Learning MOORE

When you learn any intellectual skill—either the six to eight addressed by IQ/aptitude tests or the 120 categorized by Guilford, you learn through a well-established pattern. The elements of this pattern can be neatly arranged in the MOORE Learning List. The process of learning consists of:

Motivation
Opportunity
Observation
Reinforcement
Enactment

Motivation   You won't learn anything until you're motivated to do so. This motivation can be intrinsic, satisfying an internalized need ("I really get off on this stuff"), *or* it can be extrinsic, satisfying or avoiding an external stimulus ("Hurry up and do it; here comes the stick").

There are two steps necessary to increasing your motivational levels:

1. Recognize what you control within a system.
2. Identify what benefit you will receive or what harm you will avoid as a direct result of action. (Lots of educa-

tional research verifies that when you use this identification process, the physical act of listing or note taking will increase your probability for action.)

Think about a task you know should be done, but you've managed to avoid doing—cleaning the basement, working on that back-burner project at the office, getting in touch with an aging relative, taking a training course in computer programming.

List what possible advantage or goody would come to you if you *did* the project.

List all of the horrible, nasty things that could happen to you if you *didn't* complete the task.

You need recognize only one valid point in either list to have adequate motivation to complete the task.

Opportunity   While sitting on a piano won't in itself make you another Aaron Copland, you will *never* become a genius composer/pianist if you are never in proximity to a piano. Equal opportunity in educational terms is not political jargon. It is a reality—particularily when you don't have it. Perhaps the most exciting element of opportunity is chance. (By fortunate chance, my name is not Zwiebach. Otherwise, I'd really have to stretch for an acronym.)

But you can also create opportunities for learning by the use of some good old-fashioned study habits:

- Create a "think hour." Pick one hour at any time of each day to work at any task—learning about some exciting new subject, reading, solving puzzles, increasing your vocabulary, thinking about a problem. What matters here is consistency: every day at that hour you must stop all other activity and attend to this task. Eat dinner at the same time each night and soon you'll get hungry at that time of evening. The same is true for thinking routines.
- Organize a single constant place for problem solving. This can be a favorite chair, your desk, even your car. I know one busy mother who spends from 2:00 to 3:00 P.M.

each school day parked in the pickup zone of her children's school. She keeps only blank paper and pencil in the car (no diversions such as needlepoint or *Cosmopolitan*) and uses the time to plan activities, write poetry, and outline probable solutions to current family problems.

- Even if you can't create the same think space (you're a traveling salesman), you can still associate some object with your thinking time: an old sweater, a pipe, or a soak in a tub. That silly old game of "putting on your thinking cap" works because it sets conditions for a thinking routine.

Observation Observation is metaphorical, of course, for the processing of all sensory input. If you want to learn the game of golf, you stand in your new fuzzy socks watching someone else swing the club. Yet every day we all charge past experiences, phenomena, and structures never granted this same intensity.

There is a simple but effective illustration of this principle:

1. Close your eyes and tell yourself the color of the floor of the room you are now occupying. (If you're sitting outside, any surface will do.)

2. For the rest of the day (or all day tomorrow, if you're reading this in bed) make a conscious effort to remember the color of every floor in every room you enter. Keep a pad and list each color. Note the most common and the most unusual colors.

3. For the next six days, keep track of each time you see the most common and most unusual colors. Note any really outstandingly weird floor colors.

4. On the eighth day, chart patterns of floor coverings (checkerboards, swirls, variegated colors).

5. For the next six days repeat step 3, only this time with reference to patterns.

6. On day fifteen, begin the entire process again, this time using the textures of floor surfaces.

At the end of three weeks, you will be an expert floor observer without even trying. You will never again miss anything as obvious as the color, pattern, and texture of the floor upon which you stand.

Now you're ready to move on to something more challenging. Pick another element of your environment and repeat the process. Some examples would be:

The neckties of men you encounter or the types of eyeglasses worn by coworkers

How your local professional or college team does during the season

Slang expressions, ethnic language, or accents

Price trends in the commodities markets

Reinforcement Possibly no other concept has received more educational and psychological research than this: Learning takes place in association with repeated stimuli. A few of the more significant laboratory finds since the 1930s are:

Environment reinforces behavior and shapes learning.[13]

Rewards fix habits.[14]

Punishments work about as well as do rewards in modifying behavior.[15]

A satiation of rewards or punishments will cause a waning of investigatory action.[16] (Translation: Animals get used to too much.)

An animal will respond with a desired behavior in order to avoid punishment.[17]

The more consistent the reinforcement, the more rapid the learning.[18]

But an intermittent reinforcement will result in a far more fixed—more difficult to unfix—behavior.[19] (Good news for all of you parents and office managers. Habits are more likely to form if you *don't always remember* to issue the reward or the punishment.)

Enactment Enactment is doing, and lots of enactment is practice. Both are essential for learning. Experimental psychologists call the skill *learning to learn*.

Practice strengthens perceptual association;[20] stimulates stimulus-response sequences, causing us to remember related data;[21] reinforces neurological pathways, causing subsequent enactments to occur with more ease and proficiency;[22] causes us to reorder stimuli in more efficient, more logical, and thus more likely remembered sequences.[23] Practice really does make perfect.

If you've experienced a traditional school system, you will recognize memory as one kind of intellectual skill that evolved through the MOORE learning process. In fact, within such traditional systems, learning is usually synonomous with memory display. Smart students *remember* the text. Smart students *remember* the answers to all the questions. Smart students *remember* everything that the teacher has said.

But memory is not only the retention of specific facts and tasks; it is also the retention of thinking *patterns*. A retention of thinking patterns is the elusive *capacity to learn* that IQ test makers continue to seek as an innate quality—and that is in reality a product of the learning process. (Sure would be helpful if we'd all stop painting the same horse with different colors, right?)

Let's look now at how memory is learned.

Memory: It's Not How You Take It Out— It's How You Put It In

In a highly documented case history of the last century, Jedediah Buxton, an illiterate farm laborer, carried a thirty-nine-digit number in his memory and could, at intervals, mentally multiply it by itself to arrive at the correct square. This same feat was also possible for André-Marie Ampère, the father of electrodynamics, and Carl Friedrich Gauss. One of the most brilliant mathematicians of the mid-nineteenth century, Gauss once astonished his teachers by finding the sum of the integers from 1 to 100—not by addition, but by multiplication (that's certainly enough to impress *me*).[24] Such phenomena have long been considered an *inexplicable mystery* within both the genius and severely damaged brain. For while Ampère and Gauss were eminent men of science, Jedediah Buxton was an individual whose entire memory and intellect seemed to be organized around a single precept: memorizing and multiplying those thirty-nine digits. And when such a precept is a calendar (as in the case of two highly publicized English patients), such an individual cannot process the intellectual tasks of daily living; certainly cannot compute simple mathematics; but can memorize and pinpoint the day of the week on which any date would fall in a calendar spanning forty thousand years.[25] The medical record of a similar patient stated that when taken to the theater, he sat through the entire performance apparently unmoved by the drama, only to recount later to attending physicians the total number of words spoken and steps taken by each actor in the performance.[26]

Previously, researchers suggested such incredible memory occurred because of two specifically different expressions of the same phenomenon. In the case of genius, the individual could control his/her powers of concentration and memory recall (often referred to as a photographic memory) so as to astonish those of us with normal brains. In the case of severe brain damage, the individual had been forced by extreme mental isolation to obsessively focus upon a specific precept, e.g., counting, computing square roots, understanding and using a calendar, etc. Theorists point to similar—though temporary— characteristics exhibited by isolated prisoners.

But cognitive psychologists at Carnegie-Mellon University in Pittsburgh are working to solve the mystery by *teaching* several subjects to memorize and square seemingly astronomical digit series. In the most spectacular display, Dario Donatelli is able to recall a span of numbers approaching 100! His accomplishment far exceeds the previous record held by Gauss.[27] But, rather than observing mathematical wizards or charting the behavior of extreme mental retardation, the study focuses upon subjects selected from the school's student body and judged by the researchers to have "average memory for the college student population." The Carnegie-Mellon project is succeeding because of memory techniques practiced since the beginning of human learning.

Memory is the basis of high-order cognition. You cannot analyze, evaluate, or create without a conscious recollection of past solutions and failures. I wish I could come up with something more original—but the recipe for increasing your long-term memory remains the same:

Step 1   Develop an interest in and commitment to the material to be memorized.

Step 2   Outline or organize the material into logical patterns.

Step 3   Use mnemonic association.

Step 4   Practice.

Step 5   Engage in a delayed repetition of previous input and practice.

Step 6   Recall under conditions involving emotional involvement. (Doing the real thing.)

Step 1   Develop an Interest in and Commitment to the Material to Be Memorized

Every college student knows you can sit up all night with your feet in the lavatory, cram probable test questions into your brain, successfully pass the test the next morning, and forget it all by lunchtime. Such is the fleeting nature of short-term (noncommittal) memory. But in his book *Human Intelligence,* Dr. Jack Fincher reminds us that this transitory nature of the process may be necessary for our mental well-being. "Without the full-time filtering of sensory priorities that short-term memory gives us, consciousness would be chaos."[28] (I seem to remember Mr. Spock making a similar observation in an episode of "Star Trek.")

Step 2   Outline or Organize the Material into Logical Patterns

Many studies have documented the fact that broadly significant and interconnected ideas are remembered much more easily and retained much longer than are single details.[29] *That's* where you could have screwed up on those old history tests! If, by your own personal choice, you did not learn, or if your teacher did not show you, how to organize dates and events into higher-order units, you made learning history far more difficult than it needed to be. Such a flaw in your learning pattern would also have caused you great difficulty in an IQ test.

Didn't your history teacher ever play games like this?

Organize the following words into like units:

Napoleon	approx. 1254–1324	conquest	Egypt
China	1803–1810	Exploration	Venice
French Empire	Marco Polo	Amerigo Vespucci	

Answer

Napoleon + French Empire + Egypt + conquest + 1803–1810

Marco Polo + Exploration + approx. 1254–1324 + China + Venice

(Amerigo Vespucci was somebody else altogether.)

Or what about those worksheets you completed in grade school?

Connect the words that go together:

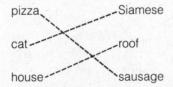

Remember those dreary English classes where the teacher insisted that you diagram sentences and write outlines? Such exercises were specifically constructed to help you begin thinking in this manner. But perhaps none of your teachers made a big deal of it—or perhaps none ever told you the significance of the event in such a way that you decided to *really* pay attention!

Step 3 Use Mnemonic Association

Sometimes called *paired associates*, mnemonic association is the linking of higher-order units to material previously stored in long-term memory.

Without turning back to chapter 2, can you remember the discussion of why people are afraid to use the skill of deductive reasoning (logic)? Two reasons for this fear were cited. What was the second? It had something to do with a guy in a gas station. If you are now making such a connection, that process is mnemonic association. It is also precisely why no teacher would *ever* present an important concept without a memorable example. And the more bizarre or unexpected the image, the better. Many educational research studies have verified that bizarre or unexpected images have stronger effect upon both immediate and delayed recall than do commonplace ones.[30] "Let me get this straight. The man you saw leaving the accident was nude and carried a frozen celery stalk?"

Mnemonic association was commonly utilized by Roman orators in a system called *loci*. In this technique, major components of a speech were associated with a habitual scene from the speaker's everyday life. If, for example, an orator walked a certain path from his home to the Forum, he would visualize that path and its landmarks, and then associate a part of his speech with something along the route. If the speech contained a reference to Caesar's exorbitant taxation policies, the orator would visualize a scene at some specific landmark in which Caesar was taking a bag of gold from a bedraggled citizen.

I had a sixth-grade teacher who, when presenting a history lesson, would tape pictures, maps, and charts to various window frames, chalkboards, and walls around the classroom. When it came time for the test, I quite naturally visualized her standing under the clock as she talked of Bull Run and moving to the wall with the pencil sharpener as she talked of Appomattox.

You call forth this technique every time you search for your lost car keys: "Now where was I when I last had those keys?"

Another classic association technique is that stalwart of education, that paragon of pedagogy—the acronym. Ever know a teacher who couldn't spout a good acronym? I, for one, remember the colors of the spectrum because of Roy G. Biv,

and can recite the sequence of the solar system because My
Very Educated Mother Just Served Us Nine Pizzas. (Red, or-
ange, yellow, green, blue, indigo, and violet. Mercury, Venus,
Earth, Mars, Jupiter, Saturn, Uranus, Neptune, and Pluto.
And now that astronomers have identified and named the new
planet MacVittee, I'll just have to adapt. The planet Mac-
Vittee? I don't think I'll be able to stand it!)

Step 4 Practice

God bless all the mothers and fathers who ever spent Mon-
day and Tuesday night drilling the kids for Wednesday morning's spelling test. It works!

Educational research has also shown that note taking and
rereading passages after a brief time period significantly increase memory recall.[31] When you're rereading those notes,
you'll find that terminal sentences are remembered most read-
ily.[32] (Every speech writer, stand-up comedian, and car salesman knows to save the kicker until the end of the presentation.)
And, with the exception of the terminal sentence, concrete sentences are recalled better than are abstract ones.[33]

Even the time of day at which input takes place can influence your memory. A 1980 British study surprised educators in
this country with the conclusion that academic material taught
in the morning resulted in superior immediate retention of *un-
important* and/or *trivial* details, while afternoon presentation
resulted in superior delayed retention of *both* trivial and major
conceptual data.[34] Therefore, the next time you want to establish a memorable event, you might try it in the afternoon.

Step 5 Engage in a Delayed Repetition of Previous Input and
Practice

Do you remember what you did *after* the big test? Walking
out of the session, heaving a sigh of relief, and chatting with
your fellow inmates—even then, you were hurriedly scanning
and recalling those bits of information of most importance to
you. "What did you put down for number seventeen?" "Who
was it who wrote 'Ode on a Grecian Urn,' anyway? Shelley or
Lord Byron?" Quickly flipping through the text—"Damn! It

was Keats. Well, I missed that one." Actually, this very inci-
dent would have been more likely permanently to resolve an association between Keats and the Urn than if you had answered
the question correctly in the first place. Teachers used to engage in the marvelous exercise of reviewing corrected test papers in class, but it seems now to be a practice in decline. I think
such decline came about as teachers began losing heart (or confidence) for the ever-ensuing academic confrontation: "What do
you mean by marking all of us wrong on number twelve? Last
week you said Dylan Thomas was a surrealist!" Pity.

The significance of delayed repetition of previous input is
also the rationale behind those review questions at the end of
textbook chapters.

Step 6   Recall under Conditions Involving Emotional
Involvement (Doing the Real Thing)

I learned the multiplication tables from ones to twenties
while reciting them before my third-grade class. We all had to
do it in turn, and it was horrifying. I can still remember who
was sitting in the front row as I fumbled through the thirteens.
But I also still remember the thirteens.

Exercises for Memory Improvement

1. *Acronyms.* Create acronyms for the following lists.
   Then use the acronyms to help you memorize the lists
   in sequence.
   a. Coccus forms of bacteria: staphylococcus, diplococ-
      cus, sarcina, and streptococcus.
   b. The eight major islands of Hawaii: Niihau, Kauai,
      Oahu, Molokai, Lanai, Maui, Kahoolawe, Hawaii.
   c. Some highlights of your femur (thigh bone): head,
      neck, greater trochanter, lesser trochanter, linea
      aspera, gluteal tubercle popliteal surface, intercon-
      dylar fossa, medial condyle, lateral condyle.
   d. Metric prefixes: exa, peta, tera, giga, mega, kilo,
      hecto, deka, deci, centi, milli, micro, nano, pico,
      femto, atto. (Hang in there—we're going to have to
      learn this stuff someday.)

2. *Paired associates.* Generate your own personalized images and words for the following digits. Memorize the phrases, memorize the digits.
Examples:
1632 = the age you get a driver's license and its double.
7619845 = the year of the American Revolutionary Spirit, Orwell's favorite year, how many nieces I have.

   a. 98576480930   **d.** 666547482
   b. 7653   **e.** 937309
   c. 6521341748726248

3. *Loci.* Make a diagram of your apartment or the first floor of your house. Note landmarks. Now look at the following list and associate each item with a landmark on an imaginary path through your home. Recite the list as you imagine a walk through your home. (You can do it. It may take a couple of tries, but you *can* do it.)

   a. binoculars   **h.** pitchfork
   b. sampan   **i.** swastika
   c. rosebush   **j.** jelly roll
   d. porcelain faucet   **k.** sinapine
   e. Scottish curling stone **l.** privet hedge
   f. seismoscope   **m.** Abu Simbel
   g. moccasin   **n.** warthog
Now make up your own list of thirty words. Try the same technique.

4. *Chaining.* Look at the following list of words. A quick way to memorize the list is to make up a chain of events using the words in sequence.

   a. fudge   **e.** geranium
   b. sunlight   **f.** pot holder
   c. Ronald Reagan **g.** thwarted
   d. promptly   **h.** instead
   A big, soft piece of fudge glistened in the sunlight. Ronald Reagan walked by and ate it. The fudge promptly made him throw up on a geranium. The only thing he had

to clean up the vomit was a blue pot holder. So, thwarted, he gave up eating and went to the Pentagon instead.

Make up your own sequence of events for the following list:

a. postmortem   e. protect
b. practically   f. pandas
c. petulant   g. plesiosaur
d. pewter

Learning Styles

Can you remember a new word after you hear it in conversation, or do you need to see it written out? Do you always touch merchandise when you browse in a gift shop—even the dumb stuff you know you'll never buy?

Experimental psychologists have noted for some time that certain animals seem to learn through a dominant sense. Cats, for example, learn most often through vision. When a box is constructed to create the optical illusion of a precipice or cliff—and a clear glass lid covers the visual abyss—a cat usually will not venture past the image of the cliff's edge. Tactile exploration would define the glass bridge, but since the cat is a visually dominant learner, it's almost always *fooled* by the illusion. Educators have extrapolated this concept, along with observations of auditory and tactile dominance in other learning experiments, and identified three major styles of learning:

- Visual learning ("See Spot run")
- Auditory learning ("Hear Spot run")
- Kinesthetic learning ("Let's all go chase Spot")

A visual learner receives information primarily through sight. The auditory learner prefers discussing or asking for instructions, and primarily listens for learning cues; while the kinesthetic learner uses tactile dominance to learn by doing.

Imagine a Christmas party in which each adult is given a microwave oven (it's a very high-achieving family). Generally, visual learners will carefully unwrap the package, peel back the plastic, and read each line of instruction before even plugging in the appliance. Auditory learners will ask everybody in the room if he or she has ever used one of these things before. Kinesthetic learners will rip open the package, plug in the micro, pop in a potato, push a couple of buttons at random, and "see how it turns out."

Since schoolwork is predominantly visual (book, notepad, test paper, chalkboard, filmstrip), it should come as no surprise that the most successful students are usually visual learners. And who later becomes the teacher? The successful student. This makes visual dominance self-perpetuating in our schools. Teachers love writing on the chalkboard, using an overhead projector, or assigning questions from the text—that's what *they* do best. Often such a visually dominant teacher will chastise a student for not "looking me in the face when I talk to you." If the kid were an auditory learner, he was simply giving the teacher his best receptor—the one on the side of his head. And God save the kinesthetic learner in this same classroom. She'll need to tear apart and reconstruct the plastic model in order to *feel* the structure of a DNA molecule.

Educators have known for some time that anything you explore with more than one sense is easier to learn. Eighty years ago in the slums of Rome, Dr. Maria Montessori theorized that so-called uneducable children would learn to recognize the alphabet more easily and faster if they used a third sense (touch) to feel the letters as well as to see and hear them. Her sandpaper cutout letters allowed the children to register tactilely and thus remember with more clarity.[35] This same principle is why kids remember songs sung to a snapping jump rope and why "Sesame Street" is so kinetic. It's why some people like moving their lips when reading, why we count on our fingers, and why, when using the telephone, we doodle bits of the conversation. It's also the reason why, when you stop at the grocery after work, you enter the store reciting aloud those items you "mustn't forget."

Regardless of your preference for learning modalities, we have much documentation regarding the final product or display of intelligence—and how it can be altered. Over and over, in countless experiments, educators and experimental psychologists have taught humans and animals to display dramatically increased intellectual functioning. And in the process, several educational researchers have observed specifically different thinking patterns in students of higher and lower intellectual display or enactment.

One study of particular importance was conducted between 1945 and 1950 at the University of Chicago. Benjamin Bloom and Lois Broder evaluated the ways in which college students solve problems.[36] They concluded (as did Bereiter and Englemann in a retest of preschoolers[37]) that failing students exhibit the following behaviors:

- One-shot thinking (guesses) as opposed to the sequential construction of probability (logic and deductive reasoning).
- An acceptance of gaps in information and comprehension. ("Who cares? That seems close enough.")
- A tendency toward subjective rather than objective proofs. ("Don't confuse me with the facts; I know how I feel.")

Bloom and Broder termed these characteristics *mental carelessness*. A glaring manifestation of this attitude, they concluded, was the skimming over or omission of instructions. But, equally important, such students failed to see each problem as a sequence of subproblems.

As a result of this and subsequent research into learning patterns of successful students, the construction of intelligence training programs (both in schools and within business and industry) have emphasized

visual learning skills
verbal comprehension skills
sequential ordering of subproblems (logic)
development of intrinsic motivation or "How to get someone to really give a damn"

GIFTED EDUCATION: THE BEST OF EDUCATIONAL TECHNOLOGY

Intellectual progress does not come from learning more of the same skill. It comes instead from learning a more efficient or more accelerated *type* of skill. The most efficient and accelerated learning skills are in a collection of techniques now called *gifted education.*

What do you recall about the tale of Peter Pan?

What was the name of Captain Hook's first mate?

These questions illustrate the two types of cognitive functioning many of us experienced during formal school days. Most often we were presented with the solutions to specific problems and asked either to interpret the problem and solution "in our own words" or to regurgitate the most acceptable solution. School was a continuous exercise in proving how well we understood and recalled known information.

While examining the ways in which intelligence is learned, Benjamin Bloom identified these two simple didactic techniques as the beginning steps in a hierarchy of six thinking skills he called the Taxonomy of Learning:[38]

Knowledge
Comprehension
Application
Analysis
Synthesis
Evaluation

Stressing the upper elements of Bloom's hierarchy is one technique educators are now employing as they teach students "to think rather than just to repeat." The following classroom discussion questions about the tale of Peter Pan illustrate the progressive learning steps represented in the taxonomy. Use them to recall and evaluate the sophistication of your own classroom experiences. What level of thinking was most representative of your intellectual education?

Bloom's Taxonomy of Learning Applied to the Tale of Peter Pan

Knowledge   Knowledge is the recognition and acquisition of specific problems and solutions. Emphasis is upon recall of the "correct" answer.

> Why did Peter first enter the Darling nursery?
> What was the name of the Indian princess?
> Who was the author of the original story?

Comprehension   Comprehension is interpretation or translation of a problem and solution into a different format. In the process, relationships and generalizations are recognized.

> In your own words, tell the conclusion of the story.
> What anthropomorphic characteristics did you see present in the character Nana (the dog)?
> Describe Tinkerbell's feelings toward Wendy.
> In reality, which character feared growing older—Peter Pan or Wendy?

Application   Application is recollection of previously acquired generalizations or solutions and application to new problems.

> In what way was the concept of motherhood relevant to the story?
> What physical laws of nature were suspended to facilitate the evolution of the story?

Analysis   Analysis is the use of deductive reasoning (formal logic), as well as general extrinsic knowledge to construct and organize a previously unknown solution.

> Does it seem reasonable that at the end of the story, a grown-up Wendy would have allowed her own daughter to fly away with Peter Pan? Is this in keeping with the play's definition of motherhood?
> Why is the role of Peter Pan always portrayed by a woman?
> If the crocodile pursuing Captain Hook had swallowed a clock (thus providing an early warning system for its presence), how would

the clock have been wound and maintained in the days before self-winding movements?

How did the pirates and the Indians come to Never-Never Land? Did they grow old?

Synthesis Synthesis is the extrapolation of elements and solutions leading to the creation of a new problem and its solution alternatives.

In an updated version of Peter Pan, what could be a modern-day equivalent of Never-Never Land?

If Peter had persuaded Wendy and her brothers to remain in Never-Never Land, what impact would they have had upon the society?

What would have happened had Captain Hook learned to fly? What would have happened had he followed Peter into the Darling nursery?

Rewrite the play as if the characters were Priscilla Pan and Wally Darling.

Please don't miss the observation that humor and comedy are often the logical extension (through analysis and synthesis) of reality into fantasy or absurdity. I think the greatest practitioners of this skill may be the Monty Python team. They take a wholly illogical premise and carry it through to its totally logical conclusion.

Evaluation Evaluation is using personal interpretations of previously learned solutions to determine the relative value of new alternatives and to judge which alternative is most appropriate to present circumstances. Thus evaluation is also subjective.

Was Peter Pan wrong to avoid growing up?

Do today's producers and directors of the play have a responsibility to negate or change the nineteenth-century concept of the stereotypic Indian warrior?

Is the play sexist in its representation of female characters?

How do dreams, such as the one experienced by Wendy, help us cope with reality?

Bloom and his colleagues felt that every concept presented in a classroom should progress along this hierarchy if a student were to learn how to solve real problems. What startled them (and subsequent educators) were observations that almost 90 percent of the classroom learning experiences they studied emphasized the patterns of knowledge and comprehension: interpreting and recounting. In addition, standardized intelligence tests demanded that a student demonstrate these simple skills, as well as (perhaps with very little prior instruction) the mid-level skills of application and analysis. Meanwhile, Bloom concluded, adult learning situations were almost exclusively composed of analysis, synthesis, and evaluation. In other words: adults spend their time solving new problems, not recalling specific details of known problems and solutions. Bloom's conclusion was that educators were spending far too much time on simplistic thinking patterns—and precious little time on developing the higher-order thinking patterns needed for future adulthood.

Predictably, his idea that schools should reverse this didactic emphasis in favor of more analysis, synthesis, and evaluation caused a bit of an academic uproar. Many educators argued that higher-order skills could be introduced only late in a child's school career. (Remember Piaget?) But most recognized a far more pragmatic objection to Bloom's recommendations. How do you think a teacher would most efficiently teach higher-order thinking skills? What vehicles would best facilitate this process? I'll give you a short list:

More essay questions on tests

Longer and more involved writing and composition exercises

More student-presentation exercises such as laboratory work, speeches, recitations or memorized passages, and long-term problem-solving projects

More opportunities for student exploration and discovery rather than mere reception of information (e.g., instead of hearing about the nineteenth-century Age of Inven-

tion, students would reconstruct simple inventions using tools of the era)
An emphasis upon research-and-retrieval skills

And just who's going to grade those thirty-five essays each
night after dinner and before "Magnum P.I."? End of debate.

Bloom's observations and suggestions were made in 1969.
In some cases the Taxonomy revolutionized school curricula, as
evidenced by the fact that instruction in higher-order thinking
patterns is now an integral part of what we term gifted education. In most schools, however, Bloom's philosophy was ignored, as the recall and repetition of correct answers continued
to occupy most classroom thinking. You must be the judge of
how your school did or did not respond to this issue.

Many instructional programs have been designed for
teaching Bloom's thinking patterns. One that most clearly sup-
plements the skills of analysis, synthesis, and evaluation is the
Critical Thinking or Problem-Solving Process. Use this technique as you work through the exercises later in this chapter.

The Problem-Solving Process

Step 1 Recognize the Problem

Obviously, you can't solve a problem until you recognize it.
Cognitive dissonance is the term describing that first mental
awareness of a problem or unresolved issue.

Step 2 Define the Problem

A common flaw in thinking sequences is an inability to define clearly the real issue. As you approach a new problem, ask
yourself the following questions.

Is this a problem that you could easily solve through trial
and error? If you're in a darkened bedroom and you must select
one matching pair of socks from a pile containing 10 white socks
and 10 black socks, your easiest path is to pick 3 socks at random; then leave the room and discard the extra sock when you
get into the light. (Two solutions are possible from this trial-
and-error approach: you could get 3 socks of one color, or you

could get 2 socks of one color and a third of a second color.)

But trial and error is much too time-consuming when the solution's possibilities are numerous (such as closing your eyes, reaching into a stuffed clothes closet, and pulling out one specific shirt).

Could you use the Proximity Technique in solving the puzzle? The classic example of this technique, a form of trial and error, is the way you could locate the central business district when you find yourself on the outskirts of a strange town: Go to an intersection and turn in the direction of the most traffic. Continue this process at each successive intersection. (This technique assumes that you're too timid to stop a native and ask for directions.)

Is this the kind of problem in which a knowledge of absolutes is the most expedient path? Trial and error can eventually lead you to the solution of a math problem, but knowing the rules of long division and/or algebra would be a far better route.

Can you break the problem into a series of subproblems?

Can you list, chart, or diagram elements into the big picture? What connections exist between known and unknown elements? Don't overlook an opportunity to verbalize your thoughts. Several researchers have concluded that "thinking aloud" or talking through a problem actually increases your ability to organize logical connections.[39] What elements have been distorted, exaggerated, diminished, or omitted?

Step 3   Is This Really *Your* Problem?

> Do you have a practical, ethical, and/or moral obligation for involvement?
> Do you have the means to carry through with a solution?
> If not, do you know who does?
> Can you influence or inform the person capable or responsible for the solution?

Step 4   Prioritize

Who says federal bureaucrats don't help the people? They've devised this perfectly wonderful word to describe the process of ordering your plan of action.

In a crisis, look for the most immediate problem. If your bathtub faucet has broken and water is running over the edge, your first problem is stopping the water—not mopping the tile. This seems apparent when discussing faucets and floors. Yet in more complex situations, we often attempt to remedy ancillary problems rather than approach the most immediate concern.

After the flood waters recede, look for the simplest sub-problem. Such a strategy can produce two benefits. First, solving the simplest problems will often increase your confidence and sense of accomplishment. Second, several simple answers can point the way to a more complex solution.

Step 5 Gather More Data

This procedure is commonly called *research and retrieval.*

Step 6 Come to a Conclusion

Making a decision can involve two distinctly different techniques: logic and reason; and intuition and gut reaction.

Logic and Reason

There are five classic models for the logical decision-making process:

1. Knocking the Alternatives
2. Ideal Solutions
3. Best Bunk for the Night
4. What If? or Scenario Writing
5. The Matrix

Knocking the Alternatives For eons, philosophers have noted the reluctance of individuals to give up a favorable decision alternative—even in exchange for another equally favorable alternative. You're having dinner in a fancy restaurant. The waiter is standing at your table with the dessert cart. Everybody else in your party has made a selection, but all of the choices look good to you. "I really would love to have a piece of that blackberry cobbler—but I love pecan pie, too. I just can't decide." Knocking the alternatives is a decision-making process in which you systematically destroy, debunk, or degrade even favorable alternatives so that you may narrow your choice to the *best*. "Every time I eat blackberries, the seeds get stuck in my front teeth. I'll take the pecan."

Ideal Solutions   List the decision alternatives. Identify the solution that would provide the greatest good for the most people. Problem: Your garden club has been given a gift of $500. Should you spend the money on:

> Remodeling the president's greenhouse
> Cash prizes for next year's Best of Garden winners
> A beer bash at the Elks Club
> "Traveling Trophies" in the form of metal garden markers to be displayed for one year in the club's grand-champion winning gardens

In this case, the "ideal solution" (the one giving the greatest amount of good to the greatest number) would probably be the traveling trophies.

Best Bunk for the Night   In this kind of decision-making process, you find yourself with several equally valuable yet quite different alternatives. Rather than selecting the best to the exclusion of the others, you find appropriate homes for all alternatives. Most educational presentations of this concept utilize something akin to the magic box of light bulbs: You have a box containing three different types of light bulbs. One type of light bulb will burn for 100 hours and cost 3¢. One will burn for 1,000 hours and cost 30¢. One will burn for one year of continuous use and cost $30. Which kind of bulb would you use? Answer: all three. Put a lot of the cheap bulbs in spots you don't use very often (attic closets, fruit cellars, etc.); put the mid-range bulb in an accessible location you use with moderate frequency (a lamp in your dining room); and put the superbulb in a continuous-use spot you don't wish to change each week (the dusk-to-dawn light, in the cupola, on the barn, near the wasp's nest).

What If? or Scenario Writing   In this process, you would take a decision alternative and extend its current parameters to *possible* consequences. What if we let a nuclear power plant locate near our town? Negative scenario: Radioactive waste could leak into our water supply; we could be inundated with money-hungry ancillary industrialists looking for cheap energy; the whole damn thing could blow up; our kids' fingers could start falling off. Positive scenario: We could get in on the ground floor and have a voice in a safety plan; we could make a lot of money when the town grows; maybe we could be the first town to do it right; we could break the backs of the Arab oil sheiks—you can't trust anybody who'd hang an oriental rug at the door of a Rolls-Royce. (This last comment is not meant to be an ethnic slur. Rather it is to illustrate a common pitfall of *futures speculation:* you can easily slip into old biases and unfounded conclusions. You hear it all the time in emotional community debates.)

The Matrix   The matrix is a graphic representation comparing decision alternatives. It can be used either with totally

Valuable Traits

Schools Available	Tui-tion Cost	Academic Quality	Social Appearance or Status	Locale
Our Town's Country Day	High	High	High—but we can't afford to keep up	Accessible
Value	−1	+1	−1	+1
Berries of the Field	Mod-erate	Hard to judge	Seems an intelligent choice	Accessible
Value	−1	−1	+1	+1
Our Lady of Perpetual Attentiveness	Low	Very high but brutal	Will please the relatives	Distant
Value	+1	−1	−1	+1
Meat and Potatoes Public	None	Can be high if you keep on top of it	Low	Near
Value	+1	+1	−1	+1

factual information, or in decisions requiring personal value judgments. Problem: I want my kids to attend the best school in town.

Intuition and Gut Reaction

Interest in formal logic has regained momentum with the growth of the computer. This has been a purely practical reformation, since the computer—solely based on logic—will not perform item number three until you tell it to perform items one and two.

Visceral intuition, or gut reaction, stands as a vague, disheveled little skill next to formal logic, but this reputation is both unfortunate and inaccurate. Rather than being a mysterious talent or a trivial emotionalism, intuition is actually an internalized collection of previous observations and associations. When called into service, this collection presents itself not as a process of intelligence, but as a product or end result. "I don't know, something just doesn't *feel* right!" More interesting, perhaps, is the way that we also label as *intuition* something as noble as the courage to leap from a logical conclusion to a *possibly* logical one. More on this point and the creative perspective in chapter 4.

Step 7 Test Your Hypothesis

Step 8 Act

Action can involve:

Generating personal momentum
Taking risks
Having the tenacity to follow a task to completion
Simply doing

In the *Mensa Genius Quiz Book*, authors Marvin Grosswirth and Dr. Abbie Salny give this advice to aspiring Mensans. "The only way to improve, enhance, and develop your intelligence is first to decide to do it and then to do it."[40]

Working Smarter Exercises

So we see that you can get genius in two ways. You can be born with an incredibly high number of dendrites—lots of chances for synaptic connection—but you can also grow your own. Thus all those pedestrian little slogans about exercising your brain as you would a muscle turn out to be physically accurate.

Adult intelligence consists of seven general thinking skill areas. Learn to function better in each, and you will become smarter than you may have ever thought possible.

IQ and aptitude tests involve elementary application of:

- visual/spatial orientation, including the reasoning skills of figural analogies
- reading comprehension, including vocabulary recognition and inference (drawing conclusions from factual clues)
- deductive reasoning (logic)

Those not addressed by standardized intelligence tests are:

- synthesis and analysis, including judgments regarding belief and nonbelief
- research and retrieval
- human relations, including interpersonal communication
- creative perspective

While these last four skills can't be easily tested, they can be perfected through training.

It's the culmination of all seven skill areas that we see as creative problem solving—the ultimate intelligence.

At this point we're no longer concerned with simple IQ or aptitude test skills. The purpose of this section is to increase your adult problem-solving abilities by exercising the last four skill areas in conjunction with more complex aspects of the first three. As you approach the exercises for each activity, follow the same basic game plan.

Step 1   Break a problem into its subcomponents.
Step 2   Analyze each component, looking for differences and similarities.
Step 3   Logically reorder the problem.
Step 4   Seek new, untried—even illogical—alternatives.
Step 5   Try a solution. If it fails, return to Step 1.

INCREASING SKILLS OF SYNTHESIS AND ANALYSIS

Benjamin Bloom defined the skills of synthesis and analysis as the ability to take a vast amount of information, organize and condense it, and then determine what elements are of most value. Furthermore, Bloom believed this ability represented one of the highest forms of intellectual accomplishment.

You begin this process in the same way you begin to comprehend a written passage.

Step 1   Get the main idea.
Step 2   Identify supporting data.
Step 3   Identify the relationship of ideas.

As you do this, you are organizing and synthesizing the data to be evaluated. You can begin to analyze the *value* of synthesized data by asking probing questions.

Regarding the author's/speaker's viewpoint:

What are the credentials of the author?
What references or sources of information were cited?
Would the author have any reason to distort truth or reality?
Can any point of view stated be totally true or totally false?

Regarding the presentation of data:

Are some facts erroneously presented as assumptions or common knowledge when they are only speculations or possibilities?

Are all ideas presented in a recognizable pattern, or are
there *hidden truths*?
Are all major statements supported with facts, reason, or
conclusions?
Can the facts presented be verified through independent
sources?
Is the logic—used to reach conclusions or elicit your acceptance to a fact—free from obvious flaws?

Synthesis and analysis, then, are the tools for real-life
problem solving and everyday creative survival. You use these
tools when you decide how to make your paycheck stretch;
when you ponder a problem with your parents or your teen-
agers; when you make some order out of chaos on your job;
when you get a community project off dead-center; when you
make people happier that you're around. Such real-life "tests"
rarely involve totally correct or totally incorrect answers. IQ
scores or grades are not given for accomplishment. Sometimes
you don't even know whether or not you've accomplished. But
it is within this higher realm of intellectual processing that
most healthy adults regularly operate. Many are even operat-
ing to genius capacity.

Read the following passage and analyze why you believe or
do not believe the main point:

There have been many theories about the demise of the dinosaurs: climatic changes, drought, flood, or a hormonal imbalance in
females of dinosaur-bearing age. Recently a new theory was proposed by geologist Walter Alvarez. While examining limestone layers
formed some sixty-five million years ago, he discovered a mysterious
clay deposit. The clay contained an extraordinarily large amount of the
element iridium. This metallic substance is rare on Earth, but common
to certain asteroids in our galaxy. Since the iridium and clay were de-
posited about the time the dinosaurs were making their earthly exit, Alvarez theorized that an asteroid had triggered the extinction of the
prehistoric reptiles.

With the help of scientists at the Lawrence Berkeley Laboratories,
Alvarez hypothesized that such an asteroid (probably six miles in di-
ameter) collided with the Earth. The result was a gigantic dust cloud.
For as many as three-to-five years, particles from this cloud would

have been held in the stratosphere. Aside from causing a hell of a mess, the dust blocked the rays of the sun, clogged plant pores, and severely inhibited pollination and spore spontaneity. Surely the dinosaurs weren't all that thrilled either. (Wonder if a stegosaurus would have snapped its head on the ground when sneezing?) At any rate, the plants died; the plant eaters died; and the meat eaters died as soon as all of those dead plant eaters began to rot. All of that probably didn't take very long.

Unlike the dinosaurs, plants could have survived the catastrophe. Seeds are so sturdy, in fact, that archaeologists have germinated wheat found within the Egyptian pyramids. After the asteroidal dust had cleared, plant start-up could have been relatively simple. Remember Mount St. Helen's? Plants sprouted through that dust in a matter of weeks.

Where could such an asteroid have hit the Earth? It should have left quite a dent. The California basin? Lake Erie? How about New Jersey? Astronomer Fred Whipple believes that it could have hit in the ocean, perhaps on a fault or continental ridge. Such an impact would have punctured the Earth's crust and tapped the lava that is spreading the continents. The result would have been a gigantic volcano and the creation of a land mass. Iceland wins the door prize. Dr. Whipple concludes that Iceland matches the geological timetable of Alvarez's suspect asteroid. And once you discard the Norse myth that states Iceland is a tooth of the slain frost giant, Ymir, the asteroid connection is as plausible as any other theory.

Always begin your analysis with Step 1: Get the main idea. The main idea of this passage is:

    a. An Asteroidal Collision
    b. How Iceland Was Formed
    c. The Alvarez Theory
    d. How the Dinosaurs Died
    e. The Whipple Theory
    f. Other _____

I chose d. How the Dinosaurs Died for the title, but you may have thought of something much better.

After excluding extraneous points, the primary format of this passage is Reverse Sequential Format (most important to least important).

Next, consider the outline. Don't feel you must always

come up with something to please your eighth-grade English teacher; just jot down a flowchart of the facts and their relationships to one another. In this outline, I've also decided to keep track of any apparent gaps in reasoning or verification of statement of fact, and conclusions made by the writer that in turn became supporting data for subsequent conclusions. These elements set the stage for later analysis.

How the Dinosaurs Died

Classification of Statement	Statement
Fact	Theories of dinosaur death: climatic changes drought flood hormonal irregularities asteroid collision
	Verification: No general resource is cited for anything in this passage, so you must assume the author has assumed that all facts are generally accepted. (More on research verification later.)
Fact	Discovery of iridium deposit: clay within 65-million-year-old limestone layers iridium rare on Earth, common on asteroids
	Verification: Once again, assumed as general knowledge.
Conclusion	Therefore, iridium came from asteroid.
Support for initial conclusion	Scientists at Berkeley agree. An astronomer has identified a probable impact site.
Speculation, based upon initial conclusion	Asteroid would have been six miles in diameter.
Support for previous speculation	Not stated, but inference is that size was calculated because of amount of clay between the layers.

Classification of Statement	Statement
Fact	Had such a collision occurred, it would have caused a gigantic dust cloud.

Verification: Here verification would seem to be a logical assumption as a result of the initial conclusion. But remember, this statement of fact may not be true, if the initial conclusion is not true.

Fact	Cloud would have lasted 3 to 5 years.

Verification: None.

Speculations	Dust blocked the sun. Blocked sun impaired plant reproduction. Some dinosaurs choked by dust.
Conclusion number 1	The ecological imbalance of the food chain resulted in dinosaur extinction.
Speculation, based upon conclusion number 2	The end was swift.
Fact	Plants were able to adapt and thus survived, while dinosaurs did not.

Verification: Verification for this fact comes in the form of two statements presented as support.

Support for previous fact	Fertile seed has been found in the Pyramids. Plants adapted quickly to layers of volcanic dust on Mount St. Helen's.
Fact	An asteroid with a diameter of 6 miles would have left a permanent scar at the impact site.

Verification: Seems to be based upon logical assumption.

Classification of Statement	Statement
Fact	Astronomer Fred Whipple says it hit the ocean.

Verification: None.

Speculation, based upon previous fact	Impact site was a fault or continental ridge.
Fact	Lava is moving the continents. Impact would have broken into lava flow.

Verification: Verification of these facts all rely directly upon the truth of each other. Such a position or hierarchy of related facts is often called a convoluted argument. If one fact falls, so do all others.

Fact used as support for final conclusion	A gigantic volcano would result in the creation of a land mass.

Verification: Probably based upon common knowledge; many people know how Hawaii was formed.

Final conclusion	Iceland was formed when asteroid hit an oceanic continental ridge.
Support for final conclusion stated as facts	Icelandic creation fits geological timetable of the dinosaur's demise. It's a good enough reason for Iceland.

Verification: None.

This passage is typical of the kinds of data you are often asked to analyze. In it, facts are presented with little or no verification, yet they could be true. In addition, logical processing is often based upon unsupported premises. "If (a) is true than (b) must be true as well."

How would you analyze this passage?

Return to the probing questions presented earlier in our discussion of analysis.

Regarding the author's viewpoint: What are the credentials of the author? In this passage, the author wasn't even identified. As with many stories you hear and read, you must decide if a decision can be made regarding the issue *without* any benefit of author credibility.

In this case, you could probably believe the passage more easily if it had been written by Alvarez (known then as the primary source) or by someone who had interviewed Alvarez (giving at least some reference to the primary source). This passage isn't even close. We must assume it was written by either a secondary source (someone who had either heard or read about the Alvarez Theory), or by someone who had created the entire episode from an imagination as fertile as those Egyptian seeds.

Would the author have had any reason to distort truth or reality? Of course, we have no way of knowing at this time. But be wary of those who sell asteroidal deflection devices.

Can the author's point of view be totally true or totally false? On the surface (no pun intended), this would appear to be true. Either the asteroid killed the dinosaurs—or it did not. But remember, this passage is presented as a theory. You are only asked to evaluate whether or not it could be a *possible truth*.

What references or sources of information were cited? Did the author tell us where he/she got this information? No. This author has assumed total responsibility for the authenticity of all facts in the passage. Therefore, the argument itself must be our means of evaluation. Can the Alvarez Theory still be evaluated? The answer is yes, even if you are not an astrogeologist or related to a scientist at the Berkeley Laboratories. Enter the noble endeavors known as research-and-retrieval skills.

INCREASING YOUR RESEARCH-AND-RETRIEVAL SKILLS

In its most basic format, research and retrieval can involve looking up words in the dictionary. But the process can also include: learning to cajole a reference librarian, being resourceful enough to contact a primary source of information, conducting original experimentation, or using the research of those experts who studied before you.

These techniques constitute great portions of those curricula known as: study skills, college/academic preparatory programs, gifted education, and cognitive training.

The following is only a partial list of ways you could begin to analyze and verify the facts presented in our dinosaur passage. Research-and-retrieval skills multiply in direct proportion to practice and self-confidence.

1. First, return to the outline and identify statements presented as common knowledge. Checking the validity of these statements can help you evaluate the accuracy and/or probability of speculations and conclusions the author presents.

Major assumptions of common knowledge within this passage:

The scientists at Lawrence Berkeley Laboratories are a credible source.

Dinosaurs are extinct.

Dust from an asteroid would have been sufficient to substantially block the sun for three to five years.

Plant- and flesh-eating dinosaurs couldn't adapt their diets when food was scarce.

Dinosaurs couldn't digest dust.

Lava is spreading the Earth's continents.

Nobody has any other explanation for Iceland.

2. Next, go to the library (or use a computer to tap into any other repository of data). If you are familiar with various scientific indexes, begin by seeking information about general topic areas: iridium, Iceland, dinosaur demise, etc. If you are not familiar with such indexes, ask the reference librarian. This glorious scholar is actually paid to help you solve mysteries.

Some avenues to research:

Try to find other volumes in which the Alvarez Theory of the death of the dinosaurs is discussed in more detail or from another viewpoint.

Have any other scientists directly challenged, refuted, or supported this theory?

What is iridium? Is it really prevalent in asteroids? Who says so?

And who is Walter Alvarez? Volumes are written describing the works and credentials of scientists. Has Alvarez been right about anything else? If not, does that rule out the possibility he could be right in this case?

Could a dust storm result from a volcano? If so, have any of them caused ecological catastrophes equivalent to the extinction of the dinosaurs?

Did plant seeds really survive within the Pyramids?

Can plants adapt to diminished sunlight? If so, how long would it take?

What kinds of plants were even around during the age of the dinosaurs?

What about this declaration concerning Iceland? Surely someone else has another theory as to how and when it was formed.

If the dinosaurs were destroyed by a catastrophe, were other plants and animals destroyed in the same event?

Who is Fred Whipple? He could be affiliated with a college or university. If so, his name and address would be listed in the *National Faculty Directory*. Or look for Dr. Whipple's professional biography in the *World Who's Who In Science*. (It's there.) Write and ask about his theory of Iceland.

How could the atmosphere or stratosphere support the weight of the dust from a gigantic asteroid? Six miles in diameter is huge!

3. Now be creative and identify other sources of information.

Call the astronomy or natural-science department of a university or museum and ask if anyone's ever heard of Alvarez's Theory.

Call or write the Lawrence Berkeley Laboratories. If they

say they're too busy to talk to you, ask if someone will at least verify what the article says about them.

If you live in a rural area, contact the local Agricultural Extension Office to see if there's anything to this seed-dormancy business.

4. Then follow up on any clue until you are either satisfied the data is sound or convinced that even if the facts may be correct, they are so speculative that you cannot make a judgment at this time.

After following all avenues of research within your power (and interest level) return to the last question regarding the process of analysis: "Is the logic used to reach conclusions or elicit your acceptance of a fact free from obvious flaws?"

In the case of our dinosaur passage, five major statements of logic were presented. Review these and determine whether or not you think they make *logical sense.*

- Iridium is rarely found on Earth.
    Iridium is found on some asteroids.
    An unusually large amount of iridium was found in the clay between two limestone layers on the Earth. Therefore, this iridium came from an asteroid.
- Without sun, plants die.
    A giganic dust cloud once blocked the sun.
    Therefore, the dust cloud caused the Earth's plants to die.
- Without plants, plant-eating dinosaurs would have died.
    Without plant-eating dinosaurs, meat-eating dinosaurs would have died.
    The plants were killed by a lack of sun.
    Therefore, the dinosaurs died.
- Dinosaurs could not have survived if their food chain had been broken.
    An asteroid and resulting dust cloud interrupted the dinosaurs' food chain.

Therefore, an asteroid caused the nonsurvival of the
dinosaurs.
• If 65 million years ago an asteroid had hit the Earth at an
underwater fault line, a volcanic land mass would have
resulted.
Iceland is a land mass formed by volcanic eruption
65 million years ago.
Therefore, Iceland is the site of an asteroid impact.

Do these syllogisms seem reasonable? In your judgment,
does the entire Alvarez theory make logical sense? If so, do you
believe it? If not, do you believe it anyway?

Do you remember the MOORE Learning List and the element of opportunity? There is a chance that in your research
you may have come upon some recent discoveries about reptiles. Several studies now conclude that temperature determines the sex of certain hatchling reptiles. Alligators and
green turtles have received the most attention. In the case of
green turtles, for example, cold temperatures (less than 28 C°)
inhibit females from hatching, while warm temperatures (more
than 29 C°) exclude almost all male turtles. A third category,
called intersex hatchlings, has also been produced at lower
temperatures.[41]

This news may not necessarily yank the cord on Alvarez.
Instead of causing a break in the food chain, an asteroid (and
resultant dust cloud) could have caused a long-term climatic catastrophe for the dinosaur. It would take only a few seasons of
unisex hatchling populations to bring an end to that tale.

But key elements in the dinosaur discussion are still far
from resolution.

BEYOND LOGIC

As you search so thoroughly for the logical conclusion,
don't overlook an opportunity to ponder totally outrageous possibilities. These ponderings evoke the skill of creative synthe-

sis and analysis: new thoughts, and fresh judgments about old
ones.

One method often used in gifted classrooms asks students
to advance scenarios or future proposals for a particular situation. Try the technique now by considering the following questions about the demise of the dinosaurs:

> What kind of a plop and tidal wave would have been caused
> by a six-mile asteroid landing in the ocean? What other
> contiguous events would have occurred? After all, we
> could be talking about *serious* fish displacement! Is this
> or any other probable phenomenon verifiable?
>
> What happened to the asteroid? Did it just dissolve in the
> ocean? Was it belched out by the volcano?
>
> Imagine a six-mile soggy asteroid being hurled out of pre-
> Iceland. Where did it go after that? (Alvarez must think
> it dried, crumbled, and became part of the volcanic
> dust.)
>
> Could some of the dinosaurs have escaped? What about air
> pockets in caves? Underwater sanctuaries? Poolside in
> the Caribbean?
>
> Were dinosaurs so dumb they couldn't learn to shake a lit-
> tle dust off the plants? Could the job have been done by
> a good wind? Could the plants have been cleaned by the
> rain?
>
> Speaking of rain . . . I thought dust made a lot of it.
>
> If the plants didn't get sunlight for three to five years, was
> the world overrun with giant mushrooms? Would giant
> mushroom patches have been sautéed when the sun fi-
> nally peered through the dust?
>
> Why weren't the insects choked to extinction? Those damn
> roaches have tiny little trachea—why didn't *they* bite
> the dust?
>
> What do you think would happen if such an asteroid hit the
> Earth today?
>
> Can you think of a way of protecting us from such an
> event?

If a new giant asteroid came, would our ICBMs automatically shoot them down? Think we should buy more, just
in case?

By what means could the iridium have arrived on Earth if
not by means of the asteroid? Could the dinosaurs have
merely been pelted with billions of small iridium-laden
asterettes? Maybe they ate them. Is anybody looking for
iridium in petrified dinosaur dung?

If the dinosaurs had not become extinct, would we have
been able to coexist with them?

Had the dinosaurs survived, would humans have evolved
at all? If so, what necessary physical and social adaptations or modifications might have occurred?

Why are people still so interested in dinosaurs, anyway?
They're gone, and good riddance, right?

What if Earth is an anteroom for the Celestial Circus of the
Cosmos? What if the dinosaurs were simply called on-
stage? What if iridium is the exhaust debris from an in-
terstellar transport? What if we're next on the bill?
Anybody got an act?

It is precisely at this point in most thinking processes that
creative synthesis and analysis leaps beyond logic. And it is
precisely because of this phenomenon that creativity and logic
are often at odds with one another in traditional academic
settings.

HUMAN-RELATIONS SKILLS

Human-relations skills in the purest sense consist of receiving and transmitting communication.

Receiving, of course, is taking in all verbal and nonverbal
cues from the behavior of others and is usually summarized as
listening skills.

The Steps for Successful Listening:

1. Empathy—caring about what the other person has to
   say.
2. Intake of data.

3. Reflecting information back for confirmation. "Then what you're really saying is . . ."
4. Asking for elaboration.

Successful transmission (usually just called *communicating*) consists of four steps:

1. Knowing yourself and what you want to say.
2. Judging the appropriateness of both action and speech. Maybe it's time for a wisecrack; maybe you need to be more serious.
3. Preparing your listener so that he or she will want to receive your message.

The way you present yourself to someone else has significant impact upon whether or not he will choose to listen to you. Obviously included in this concept are hundreds of nonverbal elements known collectively as "the first impression." These include: your physical appearance and presence, prior commitments of the listener, environmental restraints, biases, and so forth. Thousands of training techniques have been developed to address these individual factors. You're undoubtedly familiar with them; they range from dressing for success, to actual speech therapy, to combating bad breath. But in the late 1970s, Thomas Banville theorized that *the* most significant element of the communication process was not the first encounter—it was, instead, the second. How *you respond* to someone's initial communication determines whether or not he will listen to what you have to say. Banville identified five preliminary response styles that serve to inhibit or prepare a listener for receiving further communication.[42] For example, upon entering the office, the first thing a coworker says to you is: "I don't feel so good this morning. My head hurts and I feel kind of queasy."

If you respond, you will do so in one of five ways:

Interpretation: "You're probably trying to avoid that meeting with the boss."
Cross-examination: "Were you out all night, boozing?"
Reassurance: "Everybody has those days; it'll pass."

Advice giving: "If I were you, I'd go lie down."
Paraphrasing: "Having a pretty rough time, huh?"

Banville, and many other social scientists, conclude that if you want to increase the chances for further communication with this person, your best response category would be paraphrasing.

You can test this conclusion by means of a few simple communications exercises.

- Think of someone who really annoys you. (It will be even more instructive if you can't quite put your finger on the reason for such annoyance.) Engage this person in conversation. Pay particular attention to which of the five response categories he or she uses most frequently. Try the same exercise with three other dolts, fools, or clods of your acquaintance.
- Talk to three separate individuals whom you respect and admire—people you would, in fact, like to emulate. Analyze their response styles.
- If you don't mind taking a little risk, in the next five random conversations select and apply each of the five response styles. For example, when having lunch with the guys at work, concentrate on giving only interpretive responses. What reactions do you notice? Do people open up? Stop talking? Get up and change tables? Follow you back to your work station and talk some more about it?
- Select the response style with which you are most comfortable. (Maybe you will decide that you do not wish to engage in a totally "open" interpersonal communication.) Concentrate upon using it for an entire day. Two weeks later, repeat the same procedure. Make a note in your calendar to try the same experiment one month from your initial trial.

4. Presentation.

Receiving and transmitting interact in a pattern called the Successful Communication Flowchart.[43]

Successful Communication Flowchart

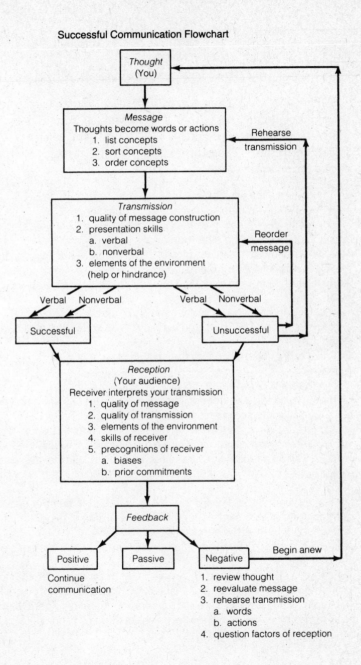

A Few More of the Thousands of Techniques for Improving Communication Skills

The following exercises will increase your awareness of how you communicate with others as well as initiate new and more effective patterns for this skill. Begin using each exercise for an entire day. Then three days. Finally, practice each exercise for an entire week.

1. Do not use the words *I, me, mine,* or *my.*
2. Every time you meet someone, ask a question.
3. In each conversation, *reflect* (repeat in your own words) major ideas expressed by the other person.
4. When someone relates an anecdote about his or her children, physical ailments, or problems getting to work—do not try to top the story. Clasp your hand over your mouth if that's the only way you can keep quiet.
5. Look people in the face when they are talking to you.
6. Find someone to whom you can say, "You know, that really was a good idea."
7. In a group interaction, ask the opinion of someone who has not yet spoken.
8. Keep track of the number of times you are able to say, "You're welcome." The inability to accept someone else's thanks or compliment is a huge block to communication.
9. In group encounters, note the reactions of others to a pause in the conversation. How do *you* feel about the silence? Anxious? Ready to jump in with an anecdote or summation? Or do you use the millisecond of silence to gather your thoughts or ponder a point in the conversation?
10. At the end of the day, list the people you can remember encountering. Make a judgment about the mood or frame of mind that characterized the nonverbal behavior of each.
11. Keep a count of how many times you interrupt when someone else is speaking.
12. As you talk to someone, try assuming and reflecting his or her tone of voice. With the next person, assume the opposite tone of voice. For example, if a coworker is yelling, respond in a calm voice. Observe and make a mental note of the response of the other person. Does he adapt to you? Persist in his tone?

13. Try the same exercise with facial expressions and physical stances.

14. Do you ever commit the cardinal sin of communication: anticipate an ending for someone's sentence, and reply with a mid-sentence rebuttal of his main point? Talk about bad form!

The final and most important thinking skill area within adult intelligence is the creative perspective. Whether using initial skills of comprehension, or more complex elements of synthesis, analysis, or communication, creative perspective is the ability to do "what works." This skill and all of its ramifications are the subject of the next chapter.

Please, God, If I Could Just Think of Something Really New

Learning Creativity

Do You Have a Creative Attitude?
(Which items do you find to be most often true?)

1. I'll try anything once, even Oysters Rancheros.
2. When I begin a project, I feel anxious until it's completed.
3. Time passes very quickly for me.
4. The best way to get something done is to do it yourself.
5. Things don't always have to be "the best" or "just right." I can usually "make do."
6. I honestly don't care what other people think. I care what I think.
7. I can't say I really have favorites. I like a little of everything.
8. I mix leftovers and heat them in the same pan.
9. I like to win, but I can get over it when I lose.
10. I like rearranging the furniture.
11. I've made some dumb mistakes in my life, but I've usually corrected them.
12. If I brought all my friends together at one party, they probably wouldn't have much in common.
13. Come to think of it, I probably wouldn't even show up for the party myself.

(*Scale:* 13 = high probability of a creative attitude. 1 = high probability of terminal herd instinct.)

IN THE FIRST PLACE, WHAT'S CREATIVITY?

Creativity is the most complex expression of intelligence—a culmination of 120 or more separate skills working in thousands of different ways. When you synthesize and analyze components of a problem until they are reformed into a workable solution, *that's* being creative. Creativity is composing a symphony or starting a small business. But it's also improvising a funny or shocking example when the prepared text of your speech is putting the audience to sleep. Creativity is doing what *works*.

How creativity occurs remains the center of great controversy. And this disagreement, like many over simpler intellectual tasks, is centered in the nature/nurture debate. Is creativity an independent and innate intellectual skill, or is it the ultimate learning experience?

Creativity Occurs as a Separate Innate Intellectual Skill (or Does It?)

In 1950, psychologist J. P. Guilford reported an extremely low correlation between IQ scores and creativity.[1] Many educators and psychologists who read the now-classic report failed to recognize that Guilford was not suggesting that intelligence and creativity were mutually exclusive and/or separate. Rather he stated that the IQ test itself failed to present tasks illustrating divergent (or creative) thinking. Ironically, Guilford's report set off a thirty-year flurry of research and verification that intelligence and creativity do not constitute the same skill.[2]

Due to this misunderstanding and its aftermath, most of the games and gimmicks now popularly associated with creativity are based upon an assumption that creativity is a separate, innate, and usually untapped skill. Some educators and social scientists categorize all intellectual activities—including creativity—and locate each within a specific brain site. Creativity, they contend, rests deep within the brain's right hemisphere. Those of us who are most creative, according to this theory, possess brains *dominated* by the right hemisphere. Meanwhile, those of us with left-dominant brains are labeled "analytical," "logical," or "noncreative." Hemispherical dominance is indeed the observable pattern for *normal* human physiology—e.g., the left side of the brain usually controls the right side of the body. But using such absolutes when defining specific sites of human intelligence leaves us with significant inconsistencies.

First, an innate brain-site/skill model does not explain those individuals discussed in chapter 3 who have apparently adapted their neurological floor plans after specific brain sites have been permanently altered by disease, trauma, or genetic malfunction. Such physical mysteries have prompted many biological anthropologists to totally abandon the functional site format in favor of more complex patterns of circuitry between brain areas.[3]

Neuroscientists probing into the mechanics of the functioning brain also dispute the specialized-site theory. Supporters of left/right brain dominance have traditionally placed logical, quantitative analytical and sequential processing—each a single element in a group of tasks labeled mathematics—in the *left* hemisphere. But during surgeries at the University of Washington, Dr. George Ojemann found at least twenty different sites on the *right* side of the brain that affect an individual's ability to multiply or divide. Dr. Ojemann discounts the theory of innate hemispherical dominance by pointing out that these supposedly specialized brain sites were not just "sitting around waiting" for the Babylonians to invent mathematics.[4]

Creativity Occurs as a Higher Level of Intellectual Functioning

The concept that creativity is a separate, innate entity is contradicted by the fact that many creative individuals regularly use and teach others to use specific strategies and procedures to induce creative products. When exploring the correlation between creative accomplishment and historically eminent geniuses, Dean Simonton concluded that intellectually creative thinkers rarely fulfilled the myth of being spontaneously *original* and *ahead of their time*. Rather, they were synthesizers who "took the accomplishments of the preceding generation and consolidated them into a single, unified philosophical system."[5] They gathered up the loose ends. True originality is usually a chance occurrence presenting itself only to that individual skillful enough to recognize it. When looking for something *really new* you can, in fact, take that which you once *knew* and transpose it to fit a need you recognize *now*.

A creative product develops as the result of:

a creative attitude, and
a process of creation

While varying in amount and style, we all display elements of each.

Those Wild and Crazy Guys: The Creative Attitude

Close your eyes and imagine a creative individual. Chances are that you would envision a male (probably bearded), a raggedy nonconformist with a Timex strapped to one biceps, an artist's brush behind one ear, and modeling clay under his fingernails. He makes strange sounds with his nose. Or perhaps you'd think of a woman with long hair, hoop earrings, and a flowing cape.

Such images don't stand the critical eye of educational and sociological research. There is significant difference between *being* creative and *acting* or *looking* creative.[6]

Being creative is not a matter of personality or appearance—it's far more a matter of attitude. With a creative attitude, you can be creative and also wear topsiders, Khaki pants (or skirt), and a navy blazer. Conversely, even if you never produce a creative thought in your life, you can still wear free-flowing clothes and whistle through your nose.

What are the attitudinal traits most often cited in research regarding creativity?

An Openness to Experience and
a Willingness to Take Risks

Apparently your ability to express these two traits comes in large measure from the degree of risk taking and the variety of experiences observed in your early environment. In one study of 278 schoolchildren, researchers concluded that the more creative children came from homes where parents were themselves involved in creative activities. In addition, the parents of these "more creative" children seemed to provide *fewer* than average—not more—materials and supplies for creative endeavors.[7] Harken! Could this mean that you may not be creative because your parents gave you too many toys, gadgets, and goodies?

If this is so, step one of becoming more creative as an adult may be the removal of instructional materials from your environment.

> *Stop* reading the label on the soup can. You can figure out which kind of sandwich goes with chicken noodle!
> *Pitch out* the directions for assembling the swing set. Experience!
> *Don't buy* the next "anything" you need; try making it for yourself—or doing without.

A study of pharmaceutical research scientists reported in the *Journal of Applied Psychology* supported a correlation between creativity in those scientists and biographical accounts of enforced decision making in childhood.[8] ("Harold, you'll just have to come up with your own science-fair project; I'm late for aerobics.")

An Internal Locus of Control and
a Positive Self-Image

Educational and psychological research consistently confirm that, in general, creative individuals resist the objections and difficulties set forth by others.[9]

To statements such as,
"You can't do that."
"We tried it before, and it didn't work."
he or she is very apt to reply, "Why the hell not?"

No task is too difficult, no challenge too remote, no problem unresolvable when you have a high self-esteem and the belief that you are in charge of your destiny. When Leonardo da Vinci was once asked to name his greatest accomplishment, he replied, "LDV."

Several researchers have discovered similarities in the early environments of other creative individuals. After interviewing eighty notably creative musicians, athletes, and mathematicians, Benjamin Bloom observed that dedication, stamina, and ability (collectively called "talent" by other scholars) were not enough to initiate or sustain their careers. Listed by these individuals were environmental factors such as: extensive family support, beginning at an early age; specialized and unique learning experiences with mentors; and a concentration of societal rewards and attention[10] (more commonly called, "the roar of the crowd").

In describing creative adults, psychologist Calvin Taylor summarizes, "They tend to have greater self-insight, self-awareness, and self-understanding by learning more about themselves. They generally have better self-concepts than others."[11]

An Attraction to Resolvable Disorder and Complexity, a Tolerance for Ambiguity, and an Ability to Concentrate or Become Absorbed in a Task

Many industrial research studies have attempted to predict just who, within a group of job applicants, would have a predilection for creative behavior. Investigations into the biographical factors and specific work habits of chemists and chemical engineers,[12] two thousand NASA scientists,[13] as well as R&D specialists selected by the Small Business Administration[14] all concluded that those individuals most likely to attack work-related problems in a creative manner showed marked preferences for:

    complex puzzles and games
    problems presenting multifaceted solution possibilities
    professional and personal goal-setting, and
    solitary and unstructured work situations

On the whole, creative workers are found to prefer complexity, display more independent judgments, and resist group pressure.[15] They also show extraordinary commitment and a high degree of success in their work.[16] One study of a team of salespersons found that high scores on standardized measurements of creativity indicated which members of the force were able to close more sales—usually by creatively overcoming customer objections.[17]

Thus the creative individual is often a highly productive, even driven worker. This contradicts the stereotypic image of a creative free spirit who works or creates whenever the urge hits him.

It's All in Knowing **How: *The Creative Process***

In addition to attitude, creativity is determined by a specific, cooperative environment—the creative process. And anyone can learn to construct it. This is most clearly illustrated by Wallas's Stages of the Creative Process.[18] In this model, every creative idea progresses through a natural order of:

1. *Preparation:* a period of data collection, problem identification, and strategy formulation.

Before Picasso created cubism, for example, he mastered the realism and artistic technique of preceding artists. He studied and learned his craft.

2. *Incubation:* time to mull things over.

Subsequent theories about the teaching of creativity suggest it is here that most of our creative ideas dissolve—we don't allow ourselves time to ponder. This is why many gifted classrooms provide a time and place in which students can simply "sit and think."

3. *Illumination:* just as the name implies—the lights go on, the bells ring, and the idea gains recognition.

4. *Verification:* testing a hypothesis.

It is at the point of verification that our environmental peers play a most crucial role:

"I just had the most terrific, unbelievable idea!"

"Sit down, fool!"

Given a degree of psychological freedom and encouragement, *every individual* can learn to create. No one espoused this with more enthusiasm than educational psychologist Carl Rogers. He believed that most of us hide creativity behind layers of social and personal intimidation, that we are fearful of ridicule, and that we therefore constantly suppress the emergence of new and unique ideas.

Rogers believed that the ability to approach *any* task with a fresh, uninhibited viewpoint could be reached only through the freedom that accompanies self-knowledge, self-assurance, and self-esteem. He thus encouraged educators to establish a sense of both psychological safety and psychological freedom in every classroom. Psychological safety is established in three ways: by showing each person his or her unconditional worth as a human being, by not judging the relative degrees and worth of creative ideas, and by showing empathetic understanding of any creative attempt. Psychological freedom, Rogers told teachers, means allowing your students total freedom of expression.[19]

How Ideas about the Creative Process Affected School Systems

First and foremost, concepts supporting the creative process were interpreted by classroom teachers to mean *environmental freedom*. This was most clearly illustrated by *open* and/or *experimental* models of classroom structure, discipline, and evaluation.

As educators studied how to implement the creative process within a classroom some interesting conclusions about performance emerged:

Students increased creative output when teachers displayed higher levels of creativity.[20]

Students increased creative output when they were simply requested to do so.[21]

A spirit of competition and reward proved to be the most effective means of teaching the creative process.[22]

These conclusions might simply be called a reaffirmation of common sense. But for the adult who questions his or her creative ability, the message is quite clear. *You can be more creative* if you will:

> Spend time with creative people.
> Find situations calling for creative behavior.
> Give yourself or find rewards for creativity.

I know many high-functioning, intelligent, socially adaptable, often creative adults who think a photo contest sponsored by the local shopping mall or a logo contest sponsored by the Kiwanis is stupid, trite, and beneath their best efforts. But educational research tells us that such exercise stimulates all levels of creativity. Creativity is just like any other human endeavor: talking about it gets you only so far!

It's All in Knowing **What: The Product Orientation**

If you want to learn to be more creative, recognizing creative products is just as essential as cultivating a creative attitude and following a creative process.

J. P. Guilford's Structure of the Intellect (SOI)[23] was the first theory to define creativity as a high level of intellectual functioning and systematically explore the products of creativity. Guilford's contribution of *how* creativity develops began with analysis of divergent thinking.

Originally he proposed that divergency was comprised of three creative products:

- *fluency*, the number of responses
    ideational fluency—rapid listing of meaningful words
    associational fluency—synonyms
    expressional fluency—putting words into organized phrases and sentences[24]
- *flexibility*, the variety of response categories
- *originality*, the uniqueness of responses

A fourth element, *elaboration* (of responses already verbalized), has been subsequently added to the theory.

We can illustrate these elements with the following problem: List some ways to bathe.

Fluency   Creative fluency would be illustrated by a great number of responses in one category, e.g.:

soak in a tub
stand in a sink
swipe with a sponge
stand under a shower
be greeted by a friendly dog
run under a waterfall
take communion in the river
wade in a mountain stream
jump in a horse trough
use a Wipe 'N Dipe
lie in an open field overnight; let the dew accumulate, and
    squeegee yourself off with a blade of Johnson grass.

Flexibility   Creative flexibility would be illustrated by a great variety of response categories, e.g.:

sunbathe
plunge into a vat of chocolate
have an Aristotelian catharsis of emotion
bathe yourself with the glory of substantial and justifiable
    praise
'fess up and come clean

Originality   Creative originality, demonstrated by novel or unique ways of approaching a problem, is rare and often the result of chance. Still, Guilford and others believed that even this skill was more likely to occur after an individual had reviewed, analyzed, and practiced the production of creative ideas. To continue with our bathing example, a unique approach might be to rearrange the letters of the problem "List some ways to bathe" so they would read: "To eat with a messy slob."

Elaboration   And, finally, *elaboration*—building upon one's responses (or the responses of others) to create a second

generation of creative products. For our ways to bathe, here is
an elaboration of creative *fluency*:

Stand naked at the zoo, spray yourself with Pam, tuck recently unrooted peanut plants in and around anatomical crev-
ices, and let a giraffe lick you clean.

We can even elaborate upon our example of *originality*.
For the British crowd, "To eat with a messy slob" can become:
"To tea with a messy slob."

But the most involved form of this concept (and the stuff of
TV sit-coms) is the elaboration of creative *flexibility*:

You and your dog, Fido, are sunning along the banks of the
Mississippi. A bully trips over your blanket and you disclose
your opinions of his mother's apparent failures with birth control. Angered, he picks you up by your shorts and dips you into
a horse trough filled with boiling Hershey's syrup. You run to
the river, jump in, and swear to high heaven that you'll change
your wicked ways if only you could be spared the pain of third-
degree burns. It doesn't work. The weight of the chocolate
pulls you into the shipping lanes. Suddenly, as if from nowhere,
Fido leaps to the rescue, extricates you from the current (just
before you would have hit the falls), throws you over his shoulder, and drags you toward the bank (almost losing it as the two
of you pass through a bed of freshwater sponges), flails you to
the land, and administers CPR. After your breathing has stabilized, he licks you clean, nestles his nose under your arm, and
whimpers in devoted empathy. God, you've found yourself one
hell of a dog!

We've all experienced Guilford's product categories in
many everyday situations. We may even have come to believe
such learning was much too much fun to have constituted gen-
uine intellectual growth. Only a lucky few can make a living at
such endeavors—and nobody ever gave you an A + for Dickie-
the-Stick and other party games. One exercise for developing
creative fluency takes form in a comic routine perfected by
Johnny Carson. During each Christmas season, Johnny por-
trays a slick TV toy salesman pushing the latest holiday necessity: Dickie-the-Stick. Dickie is actually a simple twelve-inch

pine dowel, but in the monologue Carson tells parents the many wondrous ways their children can use this marvelous toy. "Dickie-the-Stick: he's a bow and arrow for playing cowboys and Indians; he's a gun for pretend muggings; he's a probe when playing doctor. . . . That's Dickie-the-Stick! Dickie-the-Stick! Only eleven ninety-five at better department stores."

This and similar games (such as "How many words can you make out of the phrase Happy Anniversary?") have been adapted and expanded into countless classroom exercises for stimulating Guilford's creative categories.

Ways to Induce Creativity
Creative Fluency

Reverse Acronyms. Turn a four- or five-letter word into a phrase. BRATS: Bountiful Rhonda actually took second. Or, beautiful roses attract the spiders.

Greek scholars enjoyed playing number games. One involved listing "triangular" numbers: 3 ∴ and 6 ∴∴ . How many other triangular numbers can you find?

How many "square" numbers, such as 4 ∷ and 9 ∷∷ can you find?

Alternate Uses. A subtest in Guilford's Creativity Test for Children,[25] this is the educational formality of Dickie-the-Stick. How many uses can you think of for a brick? For a soda straw? For a paper clip?

Creative Flexibility

Construct at least 10 figures using a triangle △ , a rectangle ▢ a circle ○ , two straight lines ‖ , and a square ▢ . For example:

The face of a
clerk at Burger Buddies

Looking at the back of an automobile. The circle is the driver's head; the triangle is a child wearing a party hat.

A lakeside campsite

How many sentences can you construct using a different meaning for the word "spread"?

Creative Originality

To stimulate your creative originality, try *future problem solving* (E. Paul Torrance[26]). Quickly becoming one of the most popular and widespread creative techniques, future problem solving involves looking at problems (complete with ill-defined variables and unalterable conditions) and analyzing positive as well as negative scenarios. For example:

1. What are the positive and negative scenarios logically probable concerning toxic-waste disposal? Will toxic waste indeed engulf the planet, or can you imagine a solution to the problem?
2. What would happen if elementary and high schools did not dictate grade levels by chronological age?
3. How would the world be different if people had no thumbs?

Or: put a blank sheet of paper in a typewriter and come up with something.

Creative Elaboration

Combine two common items to produce a third, useful product. For example, what can you create combining a hypodermic needle with a fly on a string? (a watermelon ripeness kit)

Select fifteen to twenty words at random from the dictionary. Construct a story using all of the words. When you get really skillful, incorporate the words into one paragraph.

Draw and caption a political cartoon concerning something on today's front page.

Write an essay that begins:

You could tape bells to the toes of his shoes and pass this guy off anywhere as the court jester.

or:

What I remember most about Leona MacKenzie is how the belt to her raincoat always flapped out the bottom of her car door.

EVALUATING CREATIVITY

You may think the evaluation of creativity is something new, but in 1896 Binet had formulated open-ended, multiple-solution questions for his original test of intelligence. Unfortunately, these questions were excluded from subsequent translations and adaptations prepared for the American market. Nevertheless, in 1915 Dr. G. T. Whipple cited nineteen lesser-known tests that used questions of imagination and invention.[27]

Current assessments of creativity use the word *test* with great caution. The number, complexity, and diversity of responses—the actual creativity you seek to describe—elude simple and standardized measurement. While most evaluations of creativity focus upon the creative process and creative production, a few assess the creative attitude through opinion questionnaires and checklists (like the one that began this chapter). One such evaluation is the Something About Myself subtest of the Khatena-Torrance Creative Perception Inventory.[28] This test uses the subject's own perceptions of his environmental sensitivity, initiative, strengths, intellect, individuality, and artistry to identify creative individuals.

Sample items include:

_____ I have invented a new product.
_____ When I have an idea, I like adding to it to make it more interesting.

Evaluating the Creative Process

Such evaluation usually takes the form of behavioral observation (by a teacher or psychologist) of the creative process in action. The observer looks for:[29]

> *associational abilities:* the development of numerous and unusual associations (including puns, acronyms, and mnemonics)

analogical and metaphorical abilities: the construction of
similes, metaphors, etc. (This would also include the
ability to create a good joke.)

imagery abilities: completing figures, interpreting pictures, etc.

problem-finding abilities: the skills needed to ask relevant
questions and obtain information leading to creative behavior

Evaluating Creative Products

Researchers are still trying to develop a valid, standardized test of creative production. The following illustrate some
of their efforts.

From the Torrance Tests of Creative Thinking[30]

Ask and Guess
(An adaptation of ancient counseling techniques.)
Look at the following picture. What happened just before this
event? What will happen next?

A second implementation requires the subject to list all questions
raised—but not answered—by the picture.

Product Improvement
List several ways to change an everyday object (such as a tooth-brush) so as to make it more serviceable, aesthetic, etc.

(Guilford has devised a similar instrument, the Unusual Uses Test.)

Just Suppose
Pretend you're the President of the United States. What would you do for the first twenty-four hours you were in office? For the first month? The last twenty-four hours of your administration?

Figure Completion
Use the following incomplete figures in four separate sketches of *unusual* pictures or objects.

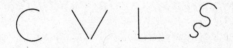

Repeated Closed Figures
Look at the six circles below. Make an object out of each.

Interpretation of this subtest varies considerably. In some trials, points are given for flexibility (more answer categories) and originality of (very unusual) answers. Six faces—even with different expressions—is about as low as you can score. Additional points are given for combining circles or extending a drawing beyond the boundaries of the actual test paper. For example, you can get lots of extra points for taping the test paper to your chest and telling people the circles are buttons on your clown suit.

From the Remote Associates Test[31]

Look at the series of 3 words and find additional words that would relate to them all.

a. Zorro   **b.** Good Hope   **c.** Red Riding Hood

Possible Answers
cape, hero, name

a. oily   **b.** dip   **c.** potato

Possible Answers
eat, chip, fry

From Flanagan's Ingenuity Tests[32]

A die-casting machine makes threading on the top of a deep metal cup that is 1 inch in diameter. However, metal chips from the threading procedure fall to the bottom of the vessel. Attempts to remove them always mar the sides. You are the design engineer. Using the clues below, which answer represents a good way of solving the problem?

a. i----p   h--h
b. m----h   c--e
c. f----r   w--l
d. l----d   b--k
e. u----e   d--n

Answer
e. thread the cup *upside down*.

You can approach this puzzle in two ways:
1. *Envision the cup-threading problem.* Gravity pulls the chips to the bottom of the vessel, so if you invert the cup, gravity will cause the chips to fall out. Look to the verbal puzzle and find the incomplete phrase that is a synonym of *invert*: u----e d--n.
2. *Attack the verbal puzzle.* Picking one simple compo-

nent, what letters could fill the spaces in d--n and thus produce a word? After much trial and error, you could deduce the words *upside down*. But many people who love and regularly practice such verbal games have (be it ever so subconsciously) trained themselves to facilitate this process with incredible speed. They can glance at the list of answer alternatives and recognize that u----e d--n represents a phrase relative to the cup-threading problem. Such a skill is not magic; it is learned.

From Torrance's Logical Reasoning Test[33]

Using only 3 lines, how could you divide a cylindrical cake into 8 sections?

Three possible solutions:

a. top view of cake   b. side view of cake   c. top view of cake

From Berger and Guilford's Plot Titles Test[34]

Read the following scenario and list possible titles for the scene: A missionary is to be boiled in oil unless he agrees to marry a cannibal princess. He refuses.

In discussing test interpretation, Guilford listed the following examples:

Poor Titles	*Better Titles*
Defeat of a Princess	Pot's Plot
Eaten by Savages	Goil or Boil
Boiled by Savages	Chaste in Haste
The Missionary Dies	A Mate Worse Than Death

Not exactly the most *objective* test you've ever seen, is it? This is precisely why nothing in the area of creativity is as controversial as the standardized evaluation of creative aptitude. While creativity tests may not be as potentially destructive as the IQ test, disagreement continues over such issues as: Should creativity evaluations be timed or untimed? (After all, a need for incubation time is a well-established concept.) Can you judge the products of creative thinking in a manner free from cultural, sexual, and/or educational bias? Should the final evaluation rest in the opinion of the society, or of the creator? And don't forget the educators and psychologists who believe with all their hearts that if it cannot be statistically validated, it cannot be true. The overriding issue in these efforts is a belief that creativity—like all other levels of intelligence—is learned. The creativity *test* serves as a stimulus for creative thought. This alone is justification enough for most educators.

DEVELOPING CREATIVITY IN BUSINESS AND INDUSTRY

Creative thinking techniques have become quite popular in that field of personnel management known as Staff (or Human Resources) Development. Grown-up versions of the same educational techniques developed in the classroom are touted to do all kinds of things in this field, especially increasing employee and managerial productivity. Some of the more popular training techniques are the following.

Word Association Training[35]

Often by means of Guilford's Unusual Uses Test or Plot Titles Test, trainees are asked over and over again to free-associate about key words and phrases. Some of these sessions can become marathons, but a great deal of clinical evidence supports the idea that when people are repeatedly asked for different word associations to the same stimulus, they will create more and more varied responses.[36]

Brainstorming

So many people have danced around ballrooms filled with brainstorming conferees that the mere mention of that odious word can bring groans from the crowd. For some reason, conference organizers think that solutions to world peace as well as lifelong friendships begin with eight total strangers brainstorming over cold taco salad. I think they even brainstorm in Brownie meetings now.

The practice survives because there are undeniable success stories. Brainstorming was created by a group of Madison Avenue advertising executives who realized that their best ideas came when they got together for a few drinks after work.[37] We could spend a dozen pages highlighting the various research studies on the subject, but it's enough to note the reason why coveys of authors, producers, and assorted ad-persons jog up to the dais at every awards ceremony: brainstorming works.[38]

Attribute Listing[39]

In this five-step process, also called *creative problem solving*, participants are taught brainstorming in order to:

1. Identify the problem.
2. Elaborate specific aspects of the problem.
3. List possible solutions to the problem.
4. Place the best possible solutions on a large grid and assign positive and negative attributes to each.
5. Implement the most positive solution by assigning the who, what, when, and where of task completion. (Always keep the grid in case your first choice doesn't work out.)

Morphological Analysis

The hallmark of advertising, this technique blends several base words or syllables to create a new word or phrase. When I was in high school a sun tanning lotion called "Tanfastic" hit the market. It could have been no more than goose grease, but with no further explanation, that name identified just what the product did.

Some of the more complex forms of morphological analysis (putting together two or more diverse concepts) are political humor, satire, and puns.

J. E. Arnold developed a series of questions to stimulate attribute listing and the morphological analysis of products. For example:

> For other uses:
>> In its present state, can it be put to other uses?
>> Can it be put to other uses if modified?
> Modification:
>> What can be added?
>> Can you duplicate or exaggerate it?
> Rearrangement:
>> Can you interchange parts?
>> Can you use a different pattern or sequence?
> Transformation:
>> Can you burn it, punch a hole in it, paint it?[40]

Metaphorical Synthesis (also called Bionics and Ideal Solutions)

I recently heard Joan Rivers spit out a brilliant metaphorical synthesis: "She's so fat, her blood type is Ragu."

There is nothing quite so dreary as analyzing a joke, but this one works because it sets up a premise (she's so fat), moves to a close association (in this case: fat/blood) and then leaps to a third, otherwise irrelevant association that is linked to the other two in two separate ways. Fat and spaghetti sauce are both associated with food. Blood and spaghetti sauce are both thick red liquids. Two additional transformations (blood to blood type and spaghetti sauce to Ragu) and a grammatical conciseness focus our attention on specifics—thus involving us more, and thus making the joke "funnier" than: "Because of an excessive amount of body fat, her blood has developed a consistency and chemical makeup resembling that of spaghetti sauce." In this form we can see that the basic premise of the joke is quite logical. We laugh because even though it seems absurd, it also seems reasonable. All of this is to say that whoever wrote the joke was using a very complex series of individual intellectual processes. The ability to do this repeatedly would even be called genius.

As a teaching technique, metaphorical synthesis involves the use of metaphors and similes to induce a creative thought. One very popular variation, developed by W. J. J. Gordon,[41] is Synectics, otherwise known as "making the familiar strange." Three examples of Synectics exercises are:

1. *Direct analogy:* How is popcorn like a flower?
2. *Personal analogy:* Imagine you are a beer can. How could your consumer be induced to keep and/or benefit from keeping you? What new design (attribute) would be of added benefit? Can you think of another form in which beer could be processed, distributed, consumed? Research beverage containers in other societies, time periods, etc. Analyze solutions as to probability of marketability, utilitarianism, etc.

This particular technique may seem silly—but Einstein said he first thought of the concept of relativity by imagining he was an elevator traveling through time.

3. *Compressed conflict:* Combining opposites to develop viewpoints. Without compressed conflict, authors could never describe a sad smile, or a brooding sunset, or how anyone can say yes and mean no.

Group Activities

These are Psychodrama, Sensitivity Training, and various other enactment techniques requiring a group coordinator. Many people fear the risk of public failure or embarrassment with these activities, although such techniques dominate the public perception of *learning to be creative.* But if you modify these popular group techniques you can become more familiar with the creative process and more comfortable with being creative. Meichenbaum's "Study of Self-Instructions,"[42] for example, employs a series of statements an individual can recite to himself before attempting a creative activity. These include: "Relax—just let it happen." "Let your ideas play." "Let your ego regress." "Pretend you are a bystander watching your ideas flow. Let one answer lead to another, and let the ideas have a life of their own."

The Futures Wheel

Based upon theories presented by Sidney Parnes, this technique uses a diagram to evaluate creativity. A specific idea, situation, or invention is placed in the center of the wheel. After all solutions have been listed, positive, negative, and neutral idea values are assigned to each solution. To complete the analysis, simply add up values and determine the most useful solution.

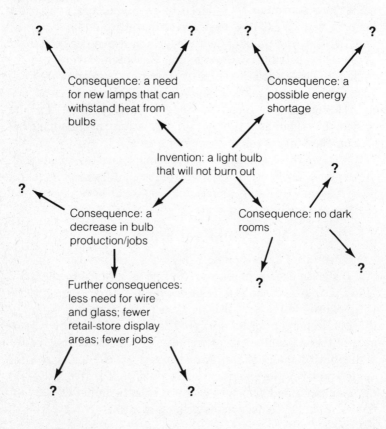

Create your own futures wheel for:

As Carl Sandburg asked, What would happen if they gave a war and nobody came?

You can become smarter, more creative, by approaching specific everyday tasks with renewed intensity. Read the following checklist and begin:

The Creativity Checklist
or How to: Be Smarter, Feel Younger, Get More Fun Out of Life, Go Further in Your Career, Make Tons of Money, and Have Better Sex

- Balance your checkbook without a calculator.
- Teach yourself to be ambidextrous. Force yourself to write notes, dial the phone, and cut your meat with your nondominant hand.
- Read the first ten pages of a trashy novel. Now complete the story yourself.
- Whenever you use dinner napkins, fold them into fancy shapes.
- Reorganize your kitchen cupboards.
- When you sit in traffic, total the numbers on neighboring license plates. Square the total. Divide by seven.
- Watch TV with the sound turned down. Deduce what is taking place. Make up your own story.
- When you go to the grocery to pick up a few things, don't make a list.
- The next time you play bridge or poker, keep track of the hand without arranging your cards into suits.
- Clip several cartoons out of magazines. Cut off the captions. Mix them up and reapply at random. Anything interesting? Does it help you think of an entirely new caption? A new cartoon?
- Make a list of the subparts of complex problems.
- Each day open a dictionary at random and read an entire page. Don't forget those strange appendixes.
- If you discover that a kid in the car pool has forgotten his swim goggles—go ahead and wear them. You know you really want to.

• The next time you go into a new city, don't take a street map. Read the signs. Look for landmarks. Make a judgment about which native you might ask.

• In a routine congregation (church, school, commuter train, sporting event), move from where you "always sit."

• Instead of eating cheese and popcorn the day before payday, create a new dish out of remnants in the refrigerator and that stuff in the back of the cupboard.

• Recite the Pledge of Allegiance backward.

• Never be without paper and pencil. As you wait behind a wreck on the expressway, sit in the dentist's reception area, or kill time during your kid's piano lesson—sketch what you see about you. It's not necessary to work toward exhibition at the National Gallery. Sketch a coffee mug on the back of a check deposit slip. Draw a chair in the margin of a magazine; see if you can put all four legs in visual perspective.

• The next time a kitchen or garden gadget breaks, don't buy a new one. Repair it or improvise.

• Follow up on curiosities. If you wonder about something—look it up, give somebody a call, ask.

• Name at least ten uses for a set of demitasse cups.

• Even if you can't afford a computer right now, find an introductory text on simple programming. If you want, skim through all the mechanics of computer circuitry and get to the core of logical progression. It's much easier than you imagined. Go to Radio Shack or the Apple store; they'll let you practice.

• Learn a second language.

• Be daring in everyday tasks. Put noodles in the baked beans.

• Every fourth time you go to the grocery, place in your cart only items that you have *never* before purchased. No cheating. No favorite snack crackers—not even your regular brand of peanut butter.

• Make anagrams out of the words on road signs.

• What is the next-to-the-last word in the Preamble to the Constitution? (Deduct 150 of your Smart Test points if you don't know what I'm talking about.)

• Recall and list all of the items in your bedroom closet.

• Pick an ad out of a magazine. How would you rewrite the copy? Improve on the graphics? Make up a new slogan for the product. Make up a better name.

- At least once a day, increase the blood flow to your brain by standing on your head, hanging your head over the edge of your bed, or throwing up over the side of a boat.

- Cut your lawn in geometric patterns—this week triangles, next week trapezoids.

- Name all fifty states and their capitals.

- Practice estimating measurements when you cook.

- When you look up a new phone number, close the book before dialing. Make yourself recall.

- If your pet's named Fido, Fluffy, or Tweety—think of a new, more descriptive name to fit its personality. Try an adjective or a verb. When you get really brave, rename your kids.

- List as many words as you can that end in *-tion*.

- Sit down and write an essay or letter to the Op-Ed page of your local newspaper. Rewrite it a couple of times before you mail it.

- Outline a story in a magazine.

- Play any game with a ball. Of particular benefit for visual/spatial orientation are: pool, handball (and assorted spinoffs), golf (Putt-Putt and otherwise).

- Learn to look at the table of contents and index every time you read a book of nonfiction. (Also note the name of the author.)

- Set goals and make a plan of action for the next five years of any long-term endeavor: your career, child rearing, your garden, or cleaning the basement.

- Even if you hate it at first, force yourself to work the crossword or anagram puzzles in the daily newspaper. Cut out the puzzle; look up the answers the next day.

- Make a list of simple elements comprising a routine task such as getting dressed or driving to the office.

- Learn to play a game of strategy: bridge, chess, Dungeons & Dragons, poker for money.

- Sing along with the car radio. Try to keep it in key. If you don't know what "in key" means, consider music lessons.

- When you're out drinking with friends and waiting for the next round, play the marriage game. For example: "If Ella Fitzgerald married Darth Vader, she'd be called . . ." (Oh, sure, those of you who can't do it will roll your eyes.)

• Take a new route home from work. Clock yourself. Compare it to previous trips.

• Every other night, sleep with your head at the foot of the bed.

• Write an essay about one of the following:
  • If there's such a thing as a swashbuckler, what's a swash?
  • How come empire starts with the letter "e" and imperial starts with the letter "i"?
  • What holds up a tree?

• How many different ways can you use a toothbrush? (To fish socks out of the sink when your nails are wet. To tickle your friends. To groom the cat. Two can be used as chopsticks.) No dessert tonight if the only thing you can come up with is "to brush your teeth."

• If you can stand the atmosphere, learn to play an arcade video game.

• Always choose parallel over diagonal parking spots. Those on the left side of one-way streets are especially good for increasing your visual/spatial perception.

• If you can't find an NPR station that will play those old radio dramas, adjust the contrast level on the TV to black. Use just the audio to deduce what's happening.

• Write a paragraph in which each successive word begins with successive letters in the alphabet: "Apparently, Belva Cornwall didn't even fathom Graham's heightened . . ."

• Open the dictionary and pick a word at random. Incorporate it into a pun. An anagram. The punchline to a humorous story. How about a complete sentence?

• Take one hour each week to walk amid the reference shelves in the public library. Look at the books.

• Watch the actors, extras, and general passersby in the backgrounds of commercials. That's where you'll find all of the real drama.

• Make a floor plan of your house or apartment. Estimate the measurements of each nook and cranny.

• Move the bushes in your yard.

• I know you won't like this one . . . but if you can find an old Latin textbook, skip the garbage on verb conjugation, and learn the chapter vocabulary drills—I promise you that your English vocabulary will soar. People tend to think you're as smart as you sound. Once everyone *thinks* that you're smarter, they'll respond to you as if you *were* smarter. Trust me. As sure as the sun, you too will rise to the occasion.

Creativity is purposeful survival. It is solving problems, constructing new ideas to benefit ourselves and others, striving to learn more—to think about things differently, to make them better. And genius, despite all its surface complexity, is simply doing just that to the utmost.

5

The Smart Test: General Enactment of Genius

If you want to lose ten pounds, I can tell you how to do it: cut out salt and eat more vegetables. And yet you won't believe me until you actually try it for a week and notice an easier closure of the clothes. Exactly the same evolution is essential if you are to learn to be more intelligent. The diet works because salt chemically causes your body to retain excess material and the fiber in veggies mechanically causes your body to expel it. Chapters 1 through 4 should have convinced you that your intellectual diet can also improve. But it's only theory until you *work* at being smarter.

Use the following checklist to evaluate any possible decline in your previously smart behavior:

The Eight Warning Signs of Smart Decline

1. You find yourself becoming intrigued with the plot of a Scooby Doo cartoon.
2. You cannot name, in succession, the U.S. Vice-Presidents who have served during your lifetime.
3. In order to give your auto license number to the attend-

ant at a self-service gas station, you have to walk to the back of the car and look at the plate.
4. You have begun to reorder the logical sequence of routine events. For example, you open the electric garage door, start the car, close the door, and back out.
5. You find yourself whistling the theme from *Mr. Rogers' Neighborhood*.
6. You always submit your Publishers' Sweepstakes card before the early-bird deadline. (Severe decline is when you actually ponder whether you'll take the cash up front, the annual income, or the house.)
7. You fall asleep during a department meeting, and nobody notices. (This is especially tragic if you're the boss.)
8. You think a punk-rock group named The Eating of the Dogs has something to do with a picnic.

The Smart Test

As we teachers love to say, "Time for your culminating activity." (That's an exercise of what you've learned so far.) Relax and have fun with this *new and improved* intelligence test.
Find the definition for the italicized words.
1. *stagnation*
   a. inactivity
   b. a rock formation
   c. a kind of fern that grows on tree bark
   d. a union of ruminants
2. *berserk*
   a. a squidlike crustacean
   b. a state of serking
   c. a bearskin worn by a Norse hero
   d. a mathematical formula
3. *juggernaut*
   a. an object of belief calling for blind devotion or sacrifice
   b. a high-flying boozer
   c. a military strategy
   d. a no-account circus performer
4. *anthesis*
   a. to reel from side to side
   b. in full bloom

        c. opposite
        d. an African mammal
   5. *pulvillus*
        a. a venereal disease
        b. a pad on an insect's foot
        c. a complex system of pulleys
        d. a Roman emperor

Find an anagram for each of the following words:
   6. loaf
   7. grips
   8. ropes

Which word completes the series?
   9. hope   open   pentacle   cleavage   ageless
        a. advantage
        b. essential
        c. close
        d. timeless
        e. breast

The words in the parenthesis were constructed by a rule. Deduce the rule and use it to fill in the blank.
  10. reside   (ideal)   dealership
        rampart   (artifact)   factitious
        imply   (?)   wooden

  11. How many months have 30 days?

  12. In a strip poker game, a shirt has the value of 1 chip, a shoe has the value of 2 chips, a hat has the value of 1 chip, and a tie has the value of 2 chips. How many chips is a blouse worth?

  13. You are the superintendent of a nuclear power plant. You've been notified that a couple of crazed anarchists have infiltrated the plant and hidden a bundle of high explosives near one of two reactor vessels. (And even a bundle of *low* explosives would ruin your day.) The vessels are on opposite sides of the plant and you have only enough time to search one area. The anarchists' psychiatrist calls to say they are in custody and will answer only one question between them. The psychiatrist warns you that one anarchist always tells the truth and the other always lies. But the anarchists are also identical twins and the psychiatrist can't tell them apart without sending a blood

test to the state capital (that would take two weeks). Which question do you ask of whom?

14. You are the owner of a small shop on a busy mall. You have seven employees. You cannot afford a part-timer for the late shift, so each of the seven must take turns staying with you until the 10:00 P.M. closing. You work late every night—but *Management Without Coronary* is another book.

Alexis wants to work the night after Cynthia because they share both an apartment and a Bulgarian boyfriend. Diana has sitter problems and can work only three nights after the night before Elaine's night. Burt insists his night to work must be three nights before Greg's because their wives trade off in a car pool to the university. Frank, your best and most senior employee, will probably quit unless he's given Thursday when his wife also works late at a shop down the mall. Besides, Thursday is halfway between Burt's night and Cynthia's night—which is good for your own mental health. What kind of schedule can you come up with? (No fair firing them all and starting over.)

Read the following passage. There *will* be a quiz.

If Men Can Be Stouthearted, Why Can't Women Have Thick Thighs?

I'm tired of being told by every magazine issue, TV hostess, and utility bill enclosure that I need to diet. Granted, I've just survived the latest three-day Wonder Fast with only a slight headache and a recurring fantasy about linguine. But, now that my body has been cleansed of sugar and my thoughts have the clarity of lemon Jell-O, I see the truth.

The truth is: I don't understand *why* I'm dieting. I don't even *like* skinny people. In the first place, they're entirely too thin. Their bones show and they have this wild and frantic look about the eyes. I think a woman looks positively disgusting when the sun shines through her thighs. I never trusted a man I outweighed.

People who diet are so pretentious. They drink Perrier and pretend it's white wine. They eat celery sticks instead of chocolate pie—and pretend they don't mind the difference. They come to your house for dinner and say things like, "Oh, nothing for me, I'm on the Scarsdale." "Was this mousse made with NutraSweet?" "We're having Oriental? I couldn't touch a thing fried."

Thin people lack aesthetic padding around otherwise grotesque parts of the human anatomy: toe joints, vertebrae, shoulder blades, and assorted angular surface areas. You don't have to take *my* word for it. Walk through any art museum. Do you honestly think Rubens would have looked twice at a woman with a protruding clavicle? Have you ever seen a portrait of a skinny queen? And don't forget that famous bit of Bombeckian wisdom: *Only a dog wants a skinny old bone.*

And what about those aerobics pimps and jogging jocks? Are they kidding? I mean, would you seriously consider patterning your behavior after some guy with a twisted nylon scarf wrapped across his forehead? Don't those people know that bottoms are supposed to bounce?

Still, we must all have some sense of social responsibility. We can't take obesity lightly. Personally, I worry about people who may someday become wedged in a booth at McLickin' Chicken. I'd vote to channel more tax dollars into the biochemical causes of true obesity. If it were up to me, stomach stapling would fall under Major Medical. There's nothing amusing about dying from fat.

But I've done my part. I've been on the all-carbohydrate, no-carbohydrate, high-protein, low-protein, the fiber-fill, and the fast. I've eaten enough grapefruit to earn a little golden tree from the Florida Citrus Growers Association. I'm just saying that millions of us who are otherwise happy and healthy are made to feel hippy and hefty. What's wrong with a size 12 (10 if the skirt's full)? Who voted 6 the regulation size?

There's a conspiracy to drive American women into starvation, and I've come to suspect everyone. Maybe it's the Russians. After we pass on to the Great Lettuce Bed, they can marry our sons to those chunky Ukrainian beauties. Maybe it's the garment industry, trying to save a few inches on each year's line. Maybe it's the AMA's master plan for getting us all back into psychiatry and away from Donahue (Phil says they don't like him). I don't know what's cookin'—but it ain't potato blintzes.

What we need is a national referendum; sort of a modern-day *call to forks.* Let us unite side to side, hip to hip, to rid ourselves of the common foe.

It's easier than you might imagine. With little change in your normal routine, you can stand up for your rights and defy those skinny, sacrilegious, self-serving dietmongers. The next time you open a can of tuna, think *real* mayonnaise. Add a few cashews for texture; serve it on a bagel. Rediscover Reese's Cups. Go to your mother's for dinner!

Who cares what Jane Fonda eats, anyway? Down with chef's salads! To hell with cottage cheese! Death to all tyrants!

Let us nurture a new awareness of the *true* body beautiful.

Strut those thighs with pride. Brandish those bellies that have borne the youth of our nation. Lift those flabby arms and cry: "God Bless You, Milton Hershey."

Without looking back through the text, answer the following questions:

15. The writer says a woman looks disgusting when
    a. she pals around with Jane Fonda
    b. eating tuna with mayo
    c. walking around an art museum
    d. the sun shines through her thighs

16. Who was not indicted by the writer in a conspiracy forcing Americans to diet?
    a. the Russians
    b. the AMA
    c. Phil Donahue
    d. the garment industry

17. What kind of diet did the writer not mention?
    a. the fiber-fill
    b. will power
    c. low carbohydrate
    d. fasting

18. What famous painter was mentioned?
    a. Bombeck
    b. Degas
    c. Rubens
    d. Perrier

19. What part of the human anatomy was not mentioned?
    a. eyes
    b. thighs
    c. clavicle
    d. toe joints

20. What clinical treatment does the writer offer the medically obese?
    a. Reese's Cups
    b. stomach stapling
    c. potato blintzes
    d. none of the above

21. In what activity was the writer engaged when the passage began?
    a. walking through an art museum
    b. surviving a fast
    c. eating
    d. reading James Beard

22. The emotion not expressed in the passage was
    a. frustration
    b. exuberance
    c. happiness
    d. paranoia (It's been promoted to the status of an emotion, hasn't it?)
23. What can you infer about the physical size of the writer?
    a. medically obese
    b. thin
    c. size 6
    d. size 12 (10 if the skirt's full)
24. What is meant when the writer uses the word *referendum*?
    a. a new diet
    b. dinner at your mother's
    c. an anti-dieting backlash
    d. a conciliator at a Brooklyn street brawl
25. Can we infer cashews are not a diet food?
    a. yes
    b. no
    c. not enough information in the text
26. The man who invented or was responsible for Hershey bars was named:
    a. Richard
    b. Milton
    c. Phil
    d. Jehovah
27. Will the writer maintain any weight loss acquired during the three-day Wonder Fast?
    a. no
    b. very unlikely
    c. are you kidding?
    d. all of the above
28. Fasting for three days has made the writer
    a. more tolerant
    b. an art lover
    c. think a lot about food
    d. appreciate large toilet stalls
29. The writer probably believes that
    a. Jane Fonda has secret passionate desires for The Galloping Gourmet
    b. Ukrainians eat a lot of lettuce

    c.   people should be judged by factors other than weight and physical appearance

    d.   despite her ravings, she needs to diet

30. What is meant by the term *the true body beautiful*?

    a.   thighs worth strutting

    b.   flabby arms

    c.   brandished bellies

    d.   all of the above

    e.   none of the above

"And now for something completely different."

31. Identify the two-dimensional figures that are the same, but are shown in different positions.

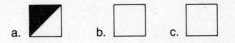

32. Complete figure **b** as a horizontal reflection of figure **a**. Complete figure **c** as a vertical reflection of figure **b**.

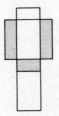

33. The outside of a box is represented below. Note the shaded sides. Which other figures *could* represent the folded and constructed box?

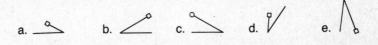

The figure below represents a solid stack of blocks. All blocks are the same size. How many blocks would have a full side in contact with each lettered block?

   34. Block A?
   35. Block B?
   36. Block C?

   37. Which of the figures below, **a** through **e**, has a dot placed so that it meets the same conditions indicated by the sample design?

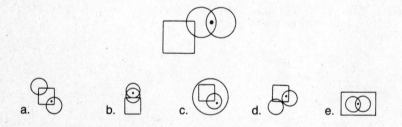

   38. You are standing in a rowboat in the middle of a calm lake. A rope is attached to the stern of the boat. If you yank on the free end of the rope, will the boat[1]:

       a. move forward?
       b. move backward?
       c. not move at all?
       d. flip out from under you?

   39. Another title for the story *Garfield Meets Beowulf* would be:
       a. "Modern Classics"
       b. "A Boy and His Cat"
       c. "Real Cats Don't Use Litter"
       d. Other: _____

40.   Look at the following stack of alphabet blocks. Each is identically lettered. Which letter is opposite the letter D?[2]

Complete the following figural analogies:

41.

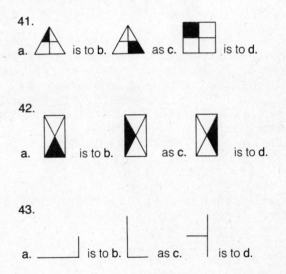

a. ⟋◺ is to b. ⟋◣ as c. ◩ is to d.

42.

a. ⧖ is to b. ◧ as c. ◨ is to d.

43.

a. ⌟ is to b. ⌞ as c. ⊤ is to d.

44.   Susan was in charge of the homemade candy booth at the PTA's Highland Fling. As always, the hit of the booth was Mrs. Bryan's giant chocolate soldiers-on-a-stick. The first three customers arrived in quick succession, each wanting to spend all his money on as many chocolate soldiers as he could. Unfortunately, the soldiers could not be equally divided. And, of course, there was no way of breaking the chocolates into portions. So Susan sold the first customer all he could afford—half of the total number plus half of a soldier. To the second customer she sold half the remaining chocolates, plus half of a soldier. To the third customer, she could sell only half of the remaining chocolate plus half of a soldier. Each customer received whole chocolate soldiers, and none were left. How many had Mrs. Bryan donated to the PTA?

45.   Which face goes with the following scenario? Aaron's team has lost the state championship, 70–0. But he's still glad since he won $98 on a 14–1 side bet.

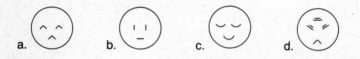

46.   Sarah, Leslie, Anne, Jessica, and Hal each have children attending the same preschool. They agree to arrange a car pool. Anne says she will drive *only* on Thursdays and that's the end of it! (She's such a pain.) Sarah is in dental school and can drive only on the day of the week that's as many days before Anne's day as Leslie's day is after Hal's. Jessica, an angel, is willing to drive any day, but she can remain in her Italian literature class if she can drive two days before Hal. Hal says that he's honestly lost interest; just give him any day. Who drives which day?

47.   Look at the following six circles and utilize each to make six separate objects.

```
O O O

O O O
```

48.   If it takes Big Ben thirty seconds to strike six o'clock, how many seconds does it take it to strike twelve o'clock? (Bet you thought I'd forgotten.)

Scoring

Your ability to keep up with the scoring of this exercise is another element of the test. Each question requires application of several intellectual skills. Thus, no scoring mechanism can facilitate those clear delineations so helpful for snappy homily. Still, each answer identifies the predominant skill represented by each question. Points will be assigned for each of six skill groups:

1. *Human Relations:* What you know about people.
2. *Deductive Reasoning:* Logic.
3. *Synthesis and Analysis:* gathering data, putting facts together, and solving a problem. This also includes research and retrieval skills.
4. *Reading Comprehension:* Complex aspects of this skill include elements of synthesis and analysis, but here we're trying to detect those elements of vocabulary recognition, simple factual and inference comprehension.
5. *Visual/Spatial Orientation:* eye/brain coordination.
6. *Creativity:* Creativity is the culmination of all knowledge, so each category involves this skill. But for scoring this test, try to identify only those times you think you've come up with a new idea.

Point values for each answer are arbitrary, but those of you with superior human-relations skills have already learned to read my biases and can surely anticipate how I may have skewed particular test questions.

Finally, you may come up with an entirely different method for solving a particular puzzle. Don't be dismayed. As long as you arrive at the same answer, give yourself full credit.

Answers

Questions 1–5: Score 7 Reading Comprehension points for each correct answer. Score 15 bonus Creativity points each time you thought of another valid definition. Add 5 Synthesis and Analysis points each time you used the dictionary. (Nobody said you couldn't use the dictionary.)

1. a.

2. c.   Actually both the bearskin and the hero carried the name. Berserk and his twelve sons (known as the Berserkers, no less) led a group of wild warriors who, in battle, would howl like wolves, growl like bears, bite their shields, and foam at the mouth.[3] And you thought the Shriners were a riot.

3. a.

4. b.   Often confused with *antithesis*, which is actually just the opposite. Deduct 5 Synthesis and Analysis points if you made this mistake.

5. b.   Trust me.

Questions 6–8: Add 20 Deductive Reasoning points for each anagram.

6.   The fun of anagrams is being snatched away by word processors capable of belching out letter patterns at lightning pace. Soon we will all have to move on to new thrills. Meanwhile, approach each anagram as a problem in deductive reasoning. Systematically explore all possible combinations of these four letters: *l-o-a-f.*

alof (Doesn't he make meat tenderizer?)
laof (the princess in *Star Wars?* No, laof—as in: "Laof what you're doin' and get out of here!")
afol (what you feel after a giant spaghetti dinner)
lafo (a great name for a clown)
lofa (as in a lofa bread)
olaf (an arcadian character in a Russian novel)
faol (a baby horse)
foal!! (the correct spelling of a baby horse)

One answer is "foal." (Add 5 additional Deductive Reasoning points each time you solved the problem in this step-by-step process. Add 10 Visual/Spatial points and 20 Synthesis and Analysis points if you were able to glance at the word and spot an instant anagram. Add 5 Creativity points each time you got sidetracked by a word association and a group of random letters.)

7. sprig

8. spore or pores (In questions 6–8, give yourself 10 additional Synthesis and Analysis credits for any other anagrams I may have missed. Give yourself 10 bonus Creativity points if you drift off into another anagram or two.)

9. **b.** essential. The last 3 letters of each word in the series are the same as the first 3 letters of the next word. Add 20 Deductive Reasoning points and 15 Synthesis and Analysis points if, as you tried to solve the puzzle, the phrase "springs eternal" kept running through your mind. (In this case your memory banks are trying to relate this new situation to "possibly pertinent" past material—even that old proverb about hope springing eternal from the human breast.)

10. The words in parenthesis contain the last 3 letters of the first words and the first 4 letters of the third words. The answer, therefore, is "ply" + "wood" = plywood. Add 50 Deductive Reasoning points for the correct answer.

11. Eleven—even though some months also have 31 days. Give yourself 35 Creativity points if you weren't fooled. (If you got it right because you've heard the joke before, this would be the same as remembering a word on a vocabulary test. Forget the Creativity points and give yourself 5 Reading Comprehension points.)

12. A blouse is worth 3 chips. Don't believe me? Start with what you know:

shirt = 1 chip
shoe   = 2 chips
hat   = 1 chip
tie   = 2 chips
blouse = ?

If you tried to assign some arbitrary value to shoes and ties based upon cost, placement on the body—whatever—you'd be making an *incorrect initial deduction*. (Remember the guy in the gas station?) If you took this path, subtract 15 Deductive Reasoning points. You may have to take such a chance later—but always begin with facts you know for certain. Look at the first 4 items of clothing and try to spot something that correlates to each chip value. In other words, try to determine the simplest possible problem—in this case, a word-game series. The word *shirt* contains 1 vowel and 4 consonants. *Shoe* contains 2 vowels and 2 consonants. . . . Right! *Blouse* contains 3 vowels and is, therefore, worth only 3 chips. (A royal rip-off, if you ask me.) You get 25 Synthesis and Analysis points for the correct answer. Add 10 Creativity points if your mind wandered to a fascinating fantasy.

13.   Assuming all nuclear-energy proponents have finished the disclaimers that no anarchist could ever penetrate a nuclear power plant, and that reactor vessels are never on opposite sides of anything; and assuming you don't waste time asking the psychiatrist just what help he's been—you may ask either twin the following:

"Which reactor vessel will your brother tell me has the explosives?" When you hear the answer, go to the other vessel.

Add 25 Deductive Reasoning points for the correct answer.

Solution: If you asked the liar, he would direct you to the vessel without the explosives. He knows that his truthful brother would tell you the truth—so the liar lies about *that* answer.

If you asked the truthful twin, he would tell you the truth: that his lying brother would lie and direct you to the vessel without the explosives.

Whichever brother you asked would direct you to the vessel without the explosives.

If you still get tangled up, try a flowchart. (Remember, you are to ask for the vessel with the explosives.)

First possibility: Ask the liar what his brother will say.

The truthful twin will identify the vessel with explosives.
The liar will counter that and tell you a lie.
You will be directed to the vessel without explosives.

Second possibility: Ask the truthful twin what his brother will say.

The liar will lie and direct you to the vessel without.
The truthful twin will tell you the truth: that his brother will identify the vessel without the explosives.

Deduct 100 Deductive Reasoning points if it never occurred to you that the anarchists could have been sisters. You should have considered this option (even if you dismissed it as having no relevance) since nothing in the test question indicated they were brothers.

14.   Begin by simplifying the problem.

Alexis the night after Cynthia. Diana can work only three nights after the night before Elaine's night. Burt's night must be three nights before Greg's. Frank must have Thursday, and Thursday is halfway between Burt's night and Cynthia's night.

You choose to placate Frank because (1) he is your best, most senior employee, (2) it would be good for you, and (3) you have to start somewhere.

Next, make a list of available facts.

Frank wants Thursday.
Frank wants equal distance from Burt and Cynthia.

—	—	—	Cynthia	Alexis
—	Elaine	—	Diana	
Burt	—	—	Greg	

Plan A

1.   Simplify more.

	C	A	
—	E	—	D
B	—	—	G

2.   Place C and A between B and G.

B	C	A	G

3.   Place F with E and D. There are two possibilities:

a.

F	E	—	D

b.

—	E	F	D

You must choose **b** because **a** will not blend with the series: B C A G.

    4.   You can combine all seven to make:

       B   C   A   G — E   F   D

       or

       — E   F   D   B   C   A   G

Plan A will not succeed because in either case Frank is not an equal distance from Burt and Cynthia.

Plan B

    1.   Simplify again by putting C and A aside. They can be added to either end of any other successful series.

    2.   Look at the remaining problem.

            F
      —   E   —   D
      B   —   —   G

    3.   Be creative. Try overlapping — E — D with B — — G. There are two possibilities:

   a. B   —   E   G   D
   b. —   E   B   D   —   G

    4.   Try fitting Frank into all three slots.

   a. B   F   E   G   D
   b. F   E   B   D   —   G
   c. —   E   B   D   F   G

Obviously, **b** must be eliminated since it does not allow contiguous slots for Cynthia and Alexis.

    5.   *So*—to review the bidding, two patterns are possible:

   a. B   F   E   G   D
   b. E   B   D   F   G

    6.   Now plug in Cynthia and Alexis (so to speak).

a.		B	F	E	G	D	C	A
b.	C	A	B	F	E	G	D
c.		E	B	D	F	G	C	A
d.	C	A	E	B	D	F	G
e.		A	E	B	D	F	G	C

    7.   Review your results:

      a.   Neither **6a, 6b,** nor **6c** will work because in neither case is Frank an equal distance from Burt and Cynthia.

b. Eureka! In all presentations of 6 **c, d, e** all factors are met and Frank is equal distance from Burt and Cynthia.

8. Frank wants Thursday; therefore:

A	E	B	D	F	G	C
|	|	|	|	|	|	|
S	M	T	W	Th	F	S

Every employee gets to work late on his chosen night. Yes, it *was* a complex managerial problem—but then that's why you get the big bucks each month.

P.S. We all know that after about a week, Cynthia and Alexis will want to switch nights.

Add 15 Deductive Reasoning points for solving the puzzle. Add 25 Creativity points if you came up with an entirely different solution.

Questions 15–21 (testing factual comprehension). Add 5 Reading Comprehension bonus points to your score each time you were able to answer without referring to the text. Add 20 Research and Retrieval bonus points for each time you ignored the instructions and looked back at the text. (In real life, people always get more bonus points for breaking rules that can't really hurt people, but can indeed solve the problem.)

15. **d.**

16. **c.**

17. **b.**

18. Even though any of these may be famous or may be a painter, only two are famous painters. And the only one of those two mentioned is **c**.

19. **a.** The writer compelled you to look at several things—but *eyes* were never mentioned.

20. **d.** While we may infer stomach stapling was offered as clinical advice to the medically obese, the statement was: "If it were up to me, stomach stapling would fall under Major Medical." And that, my friends, is what separates the rest of us from attorneys.

21. **b**

Questions 22–30 (testing inference comprehension). Add 5 Reading Comprehension points and 20 Synthesis and Analysis points for each of the following correct answers.

22. c.   Happiness is not expressed in the passage. (Actually, happiness comes later—after the pizza and before the guilt.) Frustration and paranoia seem obvious. Exuberance usually indicates intense happiness, but the word can also be used to indicate intense anger. (Add 10 Synthesis and Analysis bonus points if you took time to find the word in a dictionary. Add 5 additional Reading Comprehension points if you *remembered* the real definition of the word *exuberance*.

23. d.

24. c.

25. a.   The status of cashews as a diet food is not clearly stated, but they are included in a list of foods one should add to tuna when defying dietmongers. Even if you had never heard of cashews, you could safely infer they are not a diet food.

26. b.

27. d.   Even if you were unsure of details within the passage and even if you were to discount a *reasonable conclusion* that any food eaten after fasting would result in some weight gain—your clue is in the wording of the answer choices. Without a definite alternative answer (e.g., yes) choices **a** and **b** become the same. Since you can't absolutely define answer **c** you should assume it is also a negative. Add 20 bonus Deductive Reasoning points for this conclusion.

28. c.   The only support for any of the choices is the fact that at least twenty different foods are cited in the passage. From this we can infer the writer was thinking a lot about food.

29. d.   It would certainly be nice to assume that the writer believes people should be judged by factors other than weight and appearance. But we have no evidence or statement to support this conclusion. In fact, she seems to judge plenty of people by weight and appearance. (Subtract 50 of your Synthesis and Analysis points, as well as 50 of your Creativity points if you selected option **a**). Rather, we see a feeling of anger and persecution—coupled with a very long diet history (the no-carbohydrate, low-carbohydrate, and many others). Our safest conclusion is that the writer feels—in spite of the essay—a need to diet. Add 25 Human-Relations bonus points if you knew this without going through the analysis.

30. Since the writer uses the phrase and then gives reference to all of the following examples, we can infer the writer meant **d**, all of the above.

31. Add 25 Visual/Spatial points for figures **b** and **e**. All of the figures have been rotated. (Add 5 Synthesis and Analysis points if you reached this conclusion.) Figure **c** is excluded because of the circle on one leg. Figures **a** and **d** have legs of equal length—one half the length of the other, but **a** is a mirror image of **d**, not identical to it.

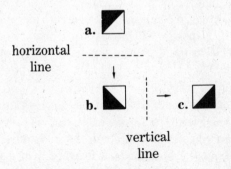

32. Your first step of this puzzle may be to translate the question by drawing the squares in the pattern requested and then following the directions.

horizontal
line

a.

b. c.

vertical
line

Horizontal reflection means rotating the figure on the horizon. (Either up or down will give you the same result.) Vertical reflection means rotating the figure on the vertical axis. (Again, either right or left.) This is a very good example of how

understanding test jargon can help your score. Add 5 Visual/
Spatial points for each correct answer.

33.   Give yourself 20 Visual/Spatial Orientation points for
each figure correctly identified. Boxes **b**, **d**, and **e** could all be
the box represented in the question. Add 50 Creativity points
if you tore a piece of paper into the large "T" shape and actually
constructed the three-dimensional box.

Questions 34–36: There are 10 blocks in the stack. You get
30 Visual/Spatial Orientation points if you spotted this imme-
diately.

34.   Block A is in contact with 2 other blocks.
35.   Block B is in full-side contact with 3 other blocks.
36.   Block C is in full-side contact with 4 other blocks.
(Two blocks cannot be seen, but must be presumed to be in
place unless a leprechaun is standing in the back corner of the
structure.) Add 35 Creativity points if, once again, you stacked
up objects to construct the relationship of the blocks.

37.   Analyze the conditions present in the first figure.
They are: a single dot within two circles and not within a
square. Under these conditions, the correct answers are **b** and
c. Each correct answer will earn you 10 Visual/Spatial points,
5 Deductive Reasoning points, and 5 Synthesis and Analysis
points.

38.   You will move the rowboat forward (answer **a**) by
yanking on the rope. The force of this yank is called inertia. It
will be strong enough to overcome the resistance of the calm
water and slightly propel the boat forward. (Once again opportunity influences intelligence. If you once had the opportunity
to go to camp, drifted to the middle of the lake during rowboat
drill, dropped your oars, noticed the rope at the boat's stern
and yanked at it in cursing desperation—then you would have
known the correct answer.)

Give yourself 20 Synthesis and Analysis points for the correct answer; 5 Reading Comprehension bonus points if you remembered about inertia.

39. Give yourself 10 Deductive Reasoning points for option **a**—it's boring, but possible; 100 Human-Relations points if you've learned enough about me to know I selected option **c**; 100 Creativity points if you thought of something better for option **d**.

40. The correct answer is S. You get 35 Visual/Spatial points if you spotted this right away; 50 Creativity points if when you became frustrated, you stacked up some three-dimensional alphabet blocks. Add 20 Visual/Spatial Macho Math points if you conjured a mental image of a flattened-out block and reshaped it.

Questions 41–43: Add 10 Visual/Spatial Orientation points and 25 Deductive Reasoning points for the correct answer.

41. (A real gift.)

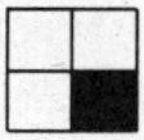

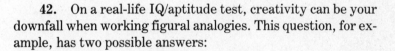

42. On a real-life IQ/aptitude test, creativity can be your downfall when working figural analogies. This question, for example, has two possible answers:

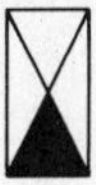 or 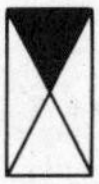

This analogy can be processed in several different ways.

If you looked at figures **a**  and **b** 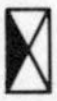 and observed that the shaded area moved from small to large, and that the position of the shaded area in figure **c** ▯ was opposite the shaded area represented in figure **b** ▯ you could have deduced that **d** ▯ should be opposite **a** ▯, or the second option ▯. Often this is reinforced by the further observation that the shaded area of the second option is the only area not represented in the first three rectangles. It therefore would represent a closure of the whole.

Or perhaps you saw the triangles of **a** ▯ and **b** ▯ together as a larger triangle on the left of the figure. This may have caused you to relate **c** ▯ to the second option ▯ as the top-to-bottom flip-flop of **a** and **b**. (But **a** and **b** together could also be a side-to-side flip-flop of the first option.) Nevertheless, you may have reasoned that your selection of the first option would mean that **a** is the same as **d**. Thus if **a** equals **b**, and **c** equals **d**, then **b** must also equal **c**. And unless you have dyslexia or severe myopia, your visual/spatial orientation should tell you that **b** does not equal **c**. Therefore, once again, you would deduce that the correct answer is the second figure. Unfortunately, all of these marvelous deductions would have led you down the wrong path.

This is because the problem does not ask you to order the four separate figures into a single whole. Instead you are to find a *relationship* between **c** and **d** that is identical to the relationship between **a** and **b**. It is easy to overlook this fundamental goal when all figures are so similar (e.g., rectangles).

Look again to **a** and **b**. The shaded area moves one space in a clockwise direction. Move the shaded area of **c** one space in a clockwise position and you will have the correct answer: ▯

IQ/aptitude-test proponents will proclaim that ambiguous items do not appear on *real* tests. Such a statement is incorrect. But far more relevant to our discussion is the fact that, in *real-life* problem-solving situations, you must constantly work around and through ambiguity.

Add 50 Creativity points and subtract 25 Deductive Reasoning points if you found both options and selected the second one.

Add 50 Creativity points and 25 Deductive Reasoning points if you found both options and selected the first one.

If you went straight for the first option, be comforted in the knowledge that you are very direct and most bright.

43.   You may have been able to glance at this problem and detect a simple rotation. If not, take it a step at a time. Analyze and list what you know of figures **a** and **b**.

Figure a:
Long horizontal line
Short vertical line
One right angle
Lines intersect at ends

Figure b:
Long vertical line
Short horizontal line
One right angle
Lines intersect at ends

Now analyze figure **c**.

Figure c:
Long vertical line
Short horizontal line
Two right angles
Lines intersect in center of long vertical

What traits can you conclude must be present in figure **d**? Since **a** and **b** have horizontal lines of opposite size:

d should have a horizontal line opposite in size to the one in **c**.

d should have a long horizontal line.

Since **a** and **b** have vertical lines of opposite size:

d should have a vertical line opposite in size to the one in **c**.

d should have a short vertical line.

Since the number, type, and placement of angles in **a** and **b** are the same:

> **d** should have two right angles intersecting the center of a long vertical line.

> At least two choices are possible:

Look to the relationship of **a** and **b** again for further data. Figure **a** rotates clockwise to form figure **b**. Rotating figure **c** clockwise, you would select the correct answer:

Add 25 Synthesis and Analysis points and 25 Deductive Reasoning points if you got it.

44.   Mrs. Byran donated seven chocolate soldiers-on-a-stick. Score 50 Deductive Reasoning points for the correct answer.

Don't be intimidated by the seeming contradiction of halves and unbroken soldiers. Look first to the *big picture*. The phrase "half of the total plus half of a soldier" is a dead giveaway that your total must be an uneven number. (Half of a number plus half to make a whole must mean the original number is not divisible by two.)

The problem is much easier if you start with the last point and work backward. If you came to this conclusion, add 50 Creativity points to your score.

   a.   The last customer bought half a soldier and half of the remaining soldiers, and none were left. Start with the simplest possible answer: 1 soldier. Add 20 additional Creativity points if at this point it occurred to you to tear a strip off the side of your test paper and rip it into little soldier representations.

   b.   Add the third customer's 1 soldier to $1/2$ to equal $1^{1}/_{2}$.

Double this number to equal 3 soldiers. The second customer had 3 soldiers available to him before his purchase. Half of the total plus $\frac{1}{2}$ equals 2 complete soldiers purchased by the second customer.

c. The first customer bought half of a soldier, plus half of the total available to him. Add the 3 soldiers involved in the other two purchases to $\frac{1}{2}$ to equal $3\frac{1}{2}$ soldiers. Double this number for a total of 7 soldiers.

Check your conclusion by reworking the problem in reverse.

a. The first customer bought $\frac{1}{2}$ of 7 (or $3\frac{1}{2}$) plus $\frac{1}{2}$ soldier for a total of 4 soldiers. That left 3 soldiers available for purchase.

b. The second customer bought $\frac{1}{2}$ of this number (or $1\frac{1}{2}$) plus $\frac{1}{2}$ for a total of 2 soldiers. That left 1 soldier.

c. The third customer bought $\frac{1}{2}$ of 1 (or $\frac{1}{2}$) plus $\frac{1}{2}$ for a total of 1 soldier.

The third customer was also Susan's cavity-prone ten-year-old, so she was thrilled with the outcome.

45. c. Give yourself 5 Visual/Spatial and 25 Human-Relations points for the correct answer.

46. Start with the one clear-cut relationship you have: Jessica driving two days before Hal.

J   —   H

Sarah wants to drive as many days before Anne as Leslie is after Hal, so you begin with the simplest combination: Sarah one day before Anne, Leslie one day after Hal.

S   A   —   H   L

But this would mean that Jessica could drive only one, not two days before Hal. Try something else.

Sarah is two days before Anne and Leslie is two days after Hal.

S   H   A   L

Eureka!

Jessica	Sarah	Hal	Anne	Leslie
|	|	|	|	|
M	T	W	Th	F

Add 20 Deductive Reasoning points for the correct answer. Add 30 Human-Relations points if you think you could have persuaded Anne to have been more flexible.

47.   Add 5 Creativity points for each completed figure.

Deduct 25 Creativity points if you drew 6 faces, 6 pieces of fruit, or 6 balls.

Add 5 additional Creativity points if when using the circle as the outer perimeter, you came up with 6 *different* figure categories. For example: a face, a soccer ball, the moon, a coin, the top view of a pie, and a clock.

Deduct 25 Creativity points if you used these same 6 categories.

Add 10 Creativity points for each figure in which you went beyond the perimeter of the circle.

For example, a flower:

Deduct 10 Creativity points if the only time you ventured out of the circle, you did indeed draw such a flower.

Add 15 bonus points if you feel any of your 6 answers is *unusual*. For example:

(A clear plastic disk sewn into a sweater so that you might display the logo of your fifty-dollar designer shirt.)

Add 150 points if you ignored the rules and incorporated all 6 circles into a larger "big picture."

For example, the top of a six-pack:

A tank:

A stack of sunglasses:

A face-to-tentacle encounter with an octopus that's trying to get out of an aquarium:

48.   Disregarding the microseconds elapsing during an actual gong, there are five intervals between gongs one and six. Thirty seconds, divided by 5, equals 6 seconds per interval. When you jump to the incorrect deduction that 6 gongs is half

of 12 gongs and so twelve o'clock should take 60 seconds—subtract 50 of your Deductive Reasoning points if you committed this blunder—you eliminate the 6-second interval between gongs six and seven. In fact, 11 intervals elapse between gongs one and twelve. That equals a total of sixty-six seconds. Add 20 Deductive Reasoning points to your score for the correct answer. Add 50 Creativity bonus points if you can think of what may have happened to that often misplaced interval between the gongs.

Add 10 bonus points for every error you may have spotted in the answer section.

Add 100 bonus points if while reading the Eight Warning Signs of Smart Decline you spotted the two characteristics that represent elements of "taste," not true intellectual decline.

Add 1,500 bonus points if at some time during the past dozen pages you stopped keeping score and concentrated upon figuring out the answers.

YOU'RE SMARTER THAN YOU THINK

I told a friend that I was writing a book about lost intelligence and the untapped potential within each of us. Her response surprised me: "My God, do you mean there's something else I have to feel guilty about not doing?"

As you worked the puzzles and games of this book—as you read about those brain-expanding rats at Berkeley—you too may have wondered if you were up to this new task. But you may already have learned more than you realize. Don't scurry around now memorizing algebraic formulas or passages from Shakespeare. Rather, take a moment to recognize your real intelligence. Think about those skills that you employ in commonplace adult problem solving:

Judging which is the best of several "terrible" solutions
Understanding what motivates and gives satisfaction to
    yourself and others

Rebounding from failure
Creating and laughing in the most adverse or mundane of
  circumstances

Such tasks are infinitely more complex than any seen on an
IQ test. And such accomplishments are what constitute a continually growing and maturing intellect.

Notes and References

1: Genius and Other Oddities

1. Leta S. Hollingworth, *Children Above 180 IQ, Stanford Binet, Origin and Development* (Yonkers, N.Y.: World, 1942).

2. Maria Montessori, *The Advanced Montessori Method* (New York: Frederick A. Stokes Co., 1917); Maria Montessori, *Dr. Montessori's Own Handbook* (New York: Schocken Books, 1965).

3. In a 1974 exploration of the latter concept, teachers from an Ohio school were asked to compile a list of their gifted students. The researchers then brought in a panel of unbiased educators familiar with gifted-education programs at other schools. A full 31 percent of those children selected by the first screening were *not* thought to be gifted by the outside panel. More to the point: of those children selected as being gifted by outside observers, 55 percent had been overlooked by their own teachers. Many studies have replicated the classic illustration of this point, the Rosenthal and Jacobson Pygmalion Effect. Psychologists Richard Rosenthal and Leonore Jacobson told the teachers of a New England high school to look for signs of rapid intellectual development in a group of select students. Supposedly the predictions came as a result of intensive IQ testing; but actually the students had been selected at random. I certainly don't want to insult your skills of deductive reasoning, but I'll give you a hint: those kids got better grades that year. See James Payne, "The Gifted," in *Behavior of Exceptional Children: An Introduction to Special Education*, ed. Norris G. Haring (Columbus, Ohio: Merrill, 1974); Richard Rosenthal and Leonore Jacobson, *Pygmalion in the Classroom:*

Teacher Expectancy and Pupils' Intellectual Development (New York: Holt, Rinehart and Winston, 1968).

4.   Milton E. Larson, in *The Gifted and the Talented,* ed. Roger Taylor (Englewood, Colo.: Educational Consulting Associates, 1975), 33.

5.   Accelerated learners (whether officially labeled as gifted or not) have been approached traditionally through accelerated curricula, enrichment, and/or ability grouping.

- *Grade or subject acceleration:* "Michelle, honey, we're going to see how you do if we move you up with the fourth graders."
- *Enrichment:* "Brian, since you: (a) scored well on our test, (b) did all your homework, or (c) jumped through any other hoop we put up, we're going to let you attend the museum's class on electromagnetism."
- *Ability Grouping:* "Hell, I don't know what to do with them! Maybe if we put them all together they'll challenge each other."

More advanced educational approaches deal directly with teaching students *how* to think and learn. Chapter 3 contains details of such problem-solving strategies, but they all have some things in common. In each, students are taught to:

Break a problem into its subcomponents
Analyze each component
Reorder the problem according to the rules of formal logic
Seek new, untried alternatives

Meanwhile, we know what happens to the gifted student in an academic environment far more elementary than his or her intellectual functioning.

Left unattended in nongifted classrooms, accelerated learners can:

- *Become disruptive, inattentive, or apathetic:* Show me a class clown and I'll show you a bright child who isn't being given appropriate learning material. Notice that I didn't say *enough* learning material. Often teachers inexperienced in gifted education feel they must keep these kids busy with huge piles of previously learned fodder. A better way to encourage growth would be to introduce less of a more intellectually challenging task.

• *Dropout:* You would recognize the names of many gifted individuals who found adult intellectual challenges far more satisfying than what was being taught in school: James Garner, Rod McKuen, Leo Tolstoy, Elaine May, Al Pacino, Colonel Harlan Sanders, Bill Mauldin, Sir Isaac Newton, Gene Hackman, and Frank Sinatra. Each was a school dropout.

When examining the records of the high school class of 1965, the state of Pennsylvania discovered more than five hundred students who had scored IQs of over 120 and then had left school before graduation. Thirty of this number had registered scores of over 130. In 1973, New York State reported 55 percent of its gifted children were underachieving, while 19 percent of the state's dropouts were classified as being gifted.

When you add to such figures statements like those from the U.S. Office of Education that IQ tests exclude as many as 50 percent of all gifted children, you can envision an even larger number of gifted dropouts.

• *Develop sloppy and inaccurate work habits:* Every teacher has observed the Stuffed Desk Syndrome. A gifted child looks at a repetitive mimeographed work sheet—goes through the motions for a few problems— then stuffs the paper away.

We adults do the same. It's called procrastination. And although some of what we put off till tomorrow is difficult and incomprehensible, most is repetitive drudge work that we know will never escape somebody's file cabinet.

The conventional wisdom has been that enduring boredom builds character. Leading a band of drunken tourists through Disney World may build character, but enduring boredom only makes you dim-witted.

- *Say, "I don't know," rather than repeat known information:* Dr. James Dunlap calls it the "revolt against rote." Often this is the gifted child's only means of retaining self-respect as he deals with a system that bores him and insults his intelligence—but in which he is totally powerless.
- *Hide abilities in order to avoid extra work:* When you were in school, how were you rewarded for completing your assignment ahead of your classmates?

  "Mary, dear, you were so quick with those algebra problems; (just for that) here are ten more."

  "Oh, I see you're finished with the geography assignment. Why don't you practice your penmanship by copying the next chapter?"

  It continues into adulthood: "I can't believe you finished that quarterly report already! How about filing away these canceled orders, by date of receipt."
- *Develop a distorted idea of what they really know:* This is the feared and often maligned "superiority complex"; it begins in a dull, unchallenging learning experience. When a child sits in a classroom, knowing all of the answers, anticipating the teacher's next question, she comes away with the idea she knows all there is to know about a given topic. Many gifted children sail through inferior high school curricula never learning to seriously work at learning. When they meet a truly challenging adult learning experience, be it higher education, a career, or the responsibilities of a family, they fail: "I guess I wasn't as smart as I thought."

See Ralph Keyes, *Is There Life after High School?* (New York: Warner Books, 1976), 45; Joseph L. French, "The Highly Intelligent Dropout," *Psychology and Education of the Gifted* (New York: Irvington, 1975), 431–32; Susanne P. Lajoie and Bruce M. Shore, "Three Myths? The Over-Representation of the Gifted among Dropouts, Delinquents and Suicides," *Gifted Child Quarterly* 25:3 (Summer 1981): 138–43; Sidney P. Marland, U.S. Commissioner of Education, Office of Education, in a report to the Congress (Washington, D.C.: Government Printing Office, 1971); James M. Dunlap, "The Education of Children with High Mental Ability," in *Education of Exceptional Children and Youth*, 3rd ed., ed. William Crickshank and G. Orville Johnson (Englewood Cliffs, N.J.: Prentice-Hall, 1975).

     6. Emily D. Stewart, "Learning Styles Among Gifted/Talented Students: Instructional Technique Preferences," *Exceptional Children* 48:2 (October 1981): 134–38.

     7. Larson, *Gifted*, 33.

     8. Alexander Wolf, "Diegophrenia and Genius," *American Journal of Psychoanalysis* 40:3 (Fall 1980): 213–26.

     9. Lots of people must believe there's something wrong with being intelligent. Parents of gifted children are continually warned about the dangers of teaching their kids *too much*. Be it injustice or downright ignorance, our society does seem to place unnecessary emotional baggage on the brightest minds. Everybody is encouraged to *do his best*, but only the gifted are given additional admonitions against *showing off*, *working ahead in the book*, and *answering too quickly*.

As a result, a gifted childhood may not have contributed greatly to an emotionally mature adulthood. Two researchers reported in the *Gifted Child Quarterly* that as a child's academic ability and IQ increase, the degree of isolation from chronological peers also increases. The suggestion is that although gifted children are not by nature antisocial, they very often cannot share their feelings and interests with classmates. This isolation is particularly intensified at early ages when the gifted child uses a vocabulary unfamiliar to other children. A verbally advanced four-year-old very often notices that the other kids don't understand what he's saying. Developmental observations tell us that all young children are emotionally self-centered. Therefore, perceived differences are apt to be interpreted with self-recrimination: "There's something wrong with me. I'm not like the other kids." Such a conclusion very often survives to chronological adulthood.

And many researchers have found that as intellectually gifted students (particularly girls!) enter adolescence, they lose peer status for being smart. In one study, J. L. Coleman interviewed students from ten diverse high schools and reported significant declines in the peer status of girls with high intelligence.

See Ann Berghout Austin and Dianne C. Draper, "Peer Relationships of the Academically Gifted," *Gifted Child Quarterly* 25:3 (Summer 1981): 129–33; J. L. Coleman, *The Adolescent Society* (New York: Free Press, 1961).

10.   Lajoie and Shore, "Three Myths?" 138–43.

11.   N. S. Caplan and M. A. Powell, "A Cross Comparison of Average to Superior IQ Delinquents," *Journal of Psychology* 57 (1964): 307–18.

12.   J. Conger et al., "Antecedents of Delinquency: Personality, Social Class and Intelligence," in *Readings in Child Development*, ed. J. Conger, P. Mussen, and J. Kagan (New York: Harper & Row, 1970); D. Gath et al., "Psychiatric and Social Characteristics of Bright Delinquents," *British Journal of Psychiatry* 116 (1970): 151–60.

13.   Hormones such as vasopressin and adrenaline seem to diminish moderate memory loss in some people. And a study reported in *Clinical Neuropsychology* suggests that blood flow to the brain *decreases* memory loss in senility patients and *increases* abstract thought processes, judgment, reasoning skills, abilities to organize information, visual/spatial processing, and sustained concentration.

For thousands of years Indian yogis have been advocating standing on your head to increase concentration. (But you should check with your doctor if you have high blood pressure.)

See Joseph T. Coyle et al., "Alzheimer's Disease: A Disorder of Cortical Cholinergic Intervention," *Science* 219:4589 (11 March 1983): 1184–90; Sharon Begley with John Carey and Ray Sawhill, "How the Brain Works," *Newsweek* (February 7, 1983): 43; Judith Rosenstock et al., "Improvement in Cognitive Functions by Increased Blood Flow to the Brain," *Clinical Neuropsychology* 2:1 (1980): 25–27.

14.   Joseph S. Bak and Roger L. Greene, "A Review of the Performance of Aged Adults on Various Wechsler Memory

Scale Subtests," *Journal of Clinical Psychology* 37:1 (January 1981): 186–88.

15. "The Brain: Holding Up Better Than We Think," *USA Today*, III: 2453, February 1983, 9.

16. Stig Berg, "Psychological Functioning in 70 and 75 Year Old People: A Study in an Industrialized City," *Acta Psychiatrica Scandinavica* 62: 288 (1980): 5–47.

17. M. Schuster and D. Barkowski, "Intelligence or Relevant Knowledge: Prerequisites for Coping Strategies in Old Age," *Zeitschrift für Gerontologie* 13:4 (1980): 385–400; Georg Rudinger and E. D. Lantermann, "Social Determinants of Intelligence in Old Age," *Zeitschrift für Gerontologie* 13:5 (September–October 1980): 403–11.

18. R. J. Alban Metcalfe, "Divergent Thinking 'Threshold Effect': IQ, Age or Skill?" *Journal of Experimental Education* 47:1 (Fall 1978).

19. H. H. Kedler and J. W. Ward, "Memory Loss Following Discrimination of Conceptually Related Material," *Journal of Experimental Child Psychology* 88 (1971): 435–36; Thomas J. Tighe, Louise S. Tighe, and Jay Schechter, "Memory for Instances and Categories in Children and Adults," *Journal of Experimental Child Psychology* 20 (1975): 22–37; Charles Liberty and Peter A. Ornstein, "Age Differences in Organization and Recall: The Effects of Training in Categorization," *Journal of Experimental Child Psychology* 15 (1973): 169–86.

20. Jo A. Lee and Robert H. Pollack, "The Effects of Age on Perceptual Problem-Solving Strategies," *Experimental Aging Research* 4:1 (February 1978): 37–54.

21. Muriel Oberledger, *Avoid the Aging Trap at 30, 50, 70* (Washington, D.C.: Acropolis, 1982).

22. Gisela Labouvie-Vief, "Dynamic Development and Mature Autonomy: A Theoretical Prologue," *Human Development* 25 (1982): 161–91.

23. Piaget's philosophy regarding early childhood became the underpinning of almost all of what we now know as formalized early and primary education—and thus had signifi-

cant impact upon the specifics of your education. For decades, only the most outrageously radical kindergarten teacher would dare introduce formal logic and deductive-reasoning skills into the lesson plan—Piaget said that kids couldn't comprehend logic until ages seven to eleven. Suffice it to say, accelerated and gifted early education have dispelled many such static chronological/developmental pigeonholes. Children, it seems, learn logic when they are appropriately taught to recognize it.

See Jean Piaget, *The Psychology of Intelligence* (London: Routledge and Kegan Paul, 1950); Herbert Ginsburg and Sylvia Opper, *Piaget's Theory of Intelligence: An Introduction* (Englewood Cliffs, N.J.: Prentice-Hall, 1969).

24.   Labouvie-Vief, "Dynamic Development," 180–90.

25.   Walter R. Cunningham, "Ability Factor Structure Differences in Adulthood and Old Age," *Multivariate Behavioral Research* 16:1 (January 1981): 3–22.

26.   J. W. Getzels and J. T. Dillon, "The Nature of Giftedness and the Education of the Gifted," in *The Gifted and the Talented*, ed. Taylor, 97–139.

27.   Lewis M. Terman et al., *Genetic Studies of Genius*, vol. 1, *Mental and Physical Traits of a Thousand Gifted Children* (Stanford, Calif.: Stanford University Press, 1926).

28.   Dorothy A. Sisk, "What If Your Child Is Gifted?" *American Education* 13:8 (October 1977): 23–26.

29.   Arthur Whimbey and Linda Shaw Whimbey, *Intelligence Can Be Taught* (New York: Bantam Books, 1975), 110.

30.   Neil Carness, "Search in Chess: Age and Skill Differences," *Journal of Experimental Psychology: Human Perception and Performance* 7:2 (April 1981): 467–76.

31.   E. Paul Torrance, "Helping Gifted Children Through Mental Health Information and Concepts," *Gifted Child Quarterly* 2 (Spring 1967): 3–7.

32.   Bryan Lindsay, "Leadership Giftedness: Developing a Profile," *Journal for the Education of the Gifted* 1:1 (February 1978): 63–69.

33.   "Renzulli/Hartman Scale for Rating Behavioral Characteristics of Superior Students," reprinted in *Exceptional Children* 38 (November 1971): 243–48.

There are also some general references for this chapter.

Guilford, Arthur M. et al. "Aspects of Language Development in the Gifted." *Gifted Child Quarterly* 25:4 (Fall 1981): 159–63.

Guilford, J. P. "Three Faces of Intellect." *American Psychologist* 14 (1959).

Meeker, Mary N. *Learning to Plan, Judge and Make Decisions: A Structure of Intellect Evaluation Workbook*. El Segundo, Calif.: SOI Institute, 1976.

Renzulli, Joseph S. "What Makes Giftedness? Reexamining a Definition." *Phi Delta Kappan*, November 1978.

Torrance, E. Paul. *Gifted Children in the Classroom*. The Psychological Foundations of Education Series (New York: Macmillan, 1965).

2: IQ

1. Leonard P. Ullmann and Leonard Krasner, eds., *A Psychological Approach to Abnormal Behavior* (Englewood Cliffs, N.J.: Prentice-Hall, 1969), 183.

2. Ibid.; Lee J. Cronbach, *Educational Psychology* (New York: Harcourt, Brace & World, 1963), 203.

3. Anne Anastasi, *Psychological Testing*. 2nd ed. (New York: Macmillan, 1961), 86.

4. Kathleen Stevens, "The Effect of Topic Interest on the Reading Comprehension of Higher Ability Students," *Journal of Educational Research* 73:6 (July–August 1980): 365–68.

5. Joseph O. Loretan, "The Decline and Fall of Group Intelligence Testing," *Teachers College Record*, October 1965.

6. Leon J. Kamin, *The Science and Politics of IQ* (New York: John Wiley & Sons, 1974), 5.

7. Ibid., 173–86.

8. Ibid., 176.

9. Stephen Jay Gould, *The Mismeasure of Man* (New York: W. W. Norton, 1981), 230–32.

10. Harry B. Gilbert, "On the IQ Ban," *Teachers College*

Record, 1966. Reprinted in Clark, *The Psychology of Education*, 54.

11.   J. A. Fishman et al., "Guidelines for Testing Minority Group Children," *Journal of Social Issues* (1964): 127–45.

12.   Gould, *Mismeasure of Man*, 265.

13.   Harold E. Mitzel, ed., *Encyclopedia of Educational Research*, 5th ed., vol. 2 (New York: Free Press, Macmillan, 1982), 939.

14.   D. C. McClelland, "Testing for Competence Rather Than for Intelligence," *American Psychologist* 28 (1972): 1–14.

15.   Mitzel, *Encyclopedia of Educational Research*, 939.

16.   Rick Heber et al., *Progress Report: Rehabilitation of Families at Risk for Mental Retardation*, Rehabilitation Research and Training Center in Mental Retardation (Madison: University of Wisconsin Press, 1972).

17.   Merle B. Karnes et al., "Effects of a Highly Structured Program of Language Development on Intellectual Functioning and Psycholinguistic Development of Culturally Disadvantaged Three-Year-Olds," *Journal of Special Education* 2 (1968): 405–12; Merle B. Karnes et al., "The Successful Implementation of a Highly Specific Preschool Instructional Program by Paraprofessional Teachers," *Journal of Special Education* 4 (1970): 69–80.

18.   Carl Bereiter and Siegfried Englemann, *Teaching Disadvantaged Children in the Preschool* (Englewood Cliffs, N.J.: Prentice-Hall, 1966).

19.   Marion Blank and Frances Solomon, "A Tutorial Language Program to Develop Abstract Thinking in Socially Disadvantaged Pre-School Children," *Child Development* (1968): 379–89.

20.   Loretan, "Group Intelligence Testing," 44.

21.   J. E. Marron, "Special Test Preparation, Its Effect on College Board Scores and the Relationship of Effected Scores to Subsequent College Performance," Office of the Director of Admissions and Registrar, U.S. Military Academy, West Point, N.Y., November 1, 1965. Mimeographed paper. See also Arthur Whimbey and Linda Shaw Whimbey, *Intelligence Can Be Taught* (New York: Bantam Books, 1975), 49–51.

22.   There are several excellent books detailing this task. I would especially recommend: Jason Millman and Walter Pauk, *How to Take Tests* (New York: McGraw-Hill, 1969).

23.   Some very interesting research and opinion in this area is beginning to emerge. For more perspective, I would suggest you read: Melvin Konner, *The Tangled Wing* (New York: Holt, Rinehart and Winston, 1982), especially chapter 6, "The Beast with Two Backs"; Elaine Morgan, *The Descent of Woman* (New York: Stein and Day, 1972)—a questioning of Charles Darwin's assumptions of which human relationship was most significant to evolution; Eleanor Emmons Maccoby and Carol Nagy Jacklin, *The Psychology of Sex Differences* (Stanford, Calif.: Stanford University Press, 1974).

24.   Robert Sternberg, "Compotential Investigations of Human Intelligence," in *Cognitive Psychology and Instruction*, ed. A. M. Lesgold et al. (New York: Plenum Press, 1978), as reported in David Lewis and James Greene, *Thinking Better* (New York: Rawson, Wade, 1982), 55.

25.   Paul J. Jacobs and Mary Vandeventer, "Evaluating the Teaching of Intelligence," *Educational and Psychological Measurement* 32 (1972), 235–48.

26.   Marvin Grosswirth and Abbie Salny, *The Mensa Genius Quiz Book* (New York: Addison-Wesley, 1981), 140.

27.   Lewis and Greene, *Thinking Better*, 78–90.

28.   Tom Burnam, *The Dictionary of Mis-Information* (New York: Thomas Y. Crowell, 1975), 79.

29.   Woody Allen, *Side Effects* (New York: Ballantine, 1980), 38.

30.   Edward Bradford Titchener, *Systematic Psychology: Prolegomena* (New York: Macmillan, 1929), 269.

31.   "Industrial Ventilation" (Paper delivered at the American Conference of Governmental Industrial Hygienists, Lansing, Mich., 1978), 13–14.

32.   S. W. Whitely and Rene Davis, "The Effects of Cognitive Intervention on Estimates of Latent Ability Measured from Analogy Items," *Technical Report*, no. 3011 (Minneapolis: University of Minnesota Press, 1973).

3: Adult Intelligence

1. J. P. Guilford, "The Structure of Intellect," *Psychology Bulletin* 53 (1956): 267–93.

2. J. P. Guilford, "Three Faces of Intellect," *American Psychologist* 14 (1959), 469–79.

3. Robert S. Albert, "Genius," in *The Encyclopedia of Clinical Assessment*, ed. R. H. Woody (San Francisco: Jossey-Bass, 1980); H. J. Butcher, *Human Intelligence: Its Nature and Assessment* (London: Methuen, 1968).

4. J. P. Guilford, *Way Beyond the IQ* (Buffalo, N.Y.: Creative Education Foundation, 1977); J. P. Guilford and R. Hoepfner, "Structure of Intellect Tests and Factors," *Reports for the Psychological Laboratory*, no. 36 (Los Angeles: University of Southern California Press, 1966).

5. J. P. Guilford, *The Nature of Human Intelligence* (New York: McGraw-Hill, 1967), 103.

6. Tiffany M. Field et al., "Discrimination and Imitation of Facial Expressions by Neonates," *Science* 218 (October 8, 1982): 179–81.

7. Melvin Konner, *The Tangled Wing* (New York: Holt, Rinehart and Winston, 1982), 404.

8. Gordon Shephard, *The Synaptic Organization of the Brain*, 2nd ed. (New York: Oxford University Press, 1979).

9. Raymond Carpenter, *Human Neuroanatomy*, 7th ed. (Baltimore, Md.: Williams and Wilkins, 1976).

10. *Newsweek*, February 7, 1983, 42; Richard M. Restak, *The Brain: The Last Frontier* (New York: Doubleday, 1979).

11. Mark R. Rosenzweig, Edward Bennett, and Marian C. Diamond, "Brain Changes in Response to Experience," *Scientific American* 226 (February 26, 1972): 22–29.

12. J. R. Conner et al., "Dendritic Increases in Aged Rat Somatosensory Cortex," *Society for Neuroscience Abstracts* 10 (1980): no. 248. 2; Rosenzweig et al., "Brain Changes," 27.

13. Henry Clay Lindgren, *Educational Psychology in the Classroom*, 3rd ed. (New York: John Wiley & Sons, 1967), 38–39.

14. Benton J. Underwood, *Experimental Psychology* (New York: Appleton-Century-Crofts, 1949), 175.

15. B. F. Skinner, *The Behavior of Organisms* (New York: Appleton-Century-Crofts, 1957).

16. J. W. Kling and L. A. Riggs, eds., *Learning, Motivation and Memory*, vol. 2 of *Woodworth and Schlosberg's Experimental Psychology*, 3rd ed. (New York: Holt, Rinehart and Winston, 1971), 588.

17. Kling and Riggs, *Learning, Motivation and Memory*, 590. Konner, *The Tangled Wing*, 386.

18. Konner, *The Tangled Wing*, 383.

19. Ibid.

20. Lee J. Cronbach, *Educational Psychology* (New York: Harcourt, Brace & World, 1963), 283–84.

21. Konner, *The Tangled Wing*, 384.

22. Konrad Lorenz, *Evolution and Modification of Behavior* (Chicago: University of Chicago Press, 1966).

23. Kling and Riggs, *Learning, Motivation and Memory*, 1043; Underwood, *Experimental Psychology*, 321.

24. Jack Fincher, *Human Intelligence* (New York: G. P. Putnam's, 1976), 305.

25. Arnold M. Rosen, "Adult Calendar Calculations in a Psychiatric OPD: A Report of Two Cases and Comparative Analysis of Abilities," *Journal of Autism and Developmental Disorders* 11:3 (September 1981): 285–92.

26. Fincher, *Human Intelligence*, 308.

27. Chris Welles, "Teaching the Brain New Tricks," *Esquire* (March 1983), 49–61.

28. Fincher, *Human Intelligence*, 33.

29. Cronbach, *Educational Psychology*, 351–52.

30. Roger Merry, "Image Bizarreness in Incidental Learning," *Psychological Reports* 46:2 (April 1980): 427–30.

31. James W. Dyer et al., "An Analysis of 3 Study Skills: Notetaking, Summarizing and Rereading," *Journal of Educational Research* 73:1 (September–October 1979): 3–7.

32. Kazuko Kojo, "The Effects of Imagery in Sentence Memory: The Recall of Concrete and Abstract Sentences," *Journal of Psychology* 50:3 (August 1979): 153–56.

33. Ibid., 156.

34. Simon Folkard, "A Note on Time of Day Effects In

School Children's Immediate and Delayed Recall of Meaningful Material," *British Journal of Psychology* 71:1 (February 1980) 95–97.

35.   Maria Montessori, *Dr. Montessori's Own Handbook* (New York: Schocken Books, 1965).

36.   Benjamin Bloom and Lois Broder, *The Problem Solving Processes of College Students* (Chicago: University of Chicago Press, 1950).

37.   Carl Bereiter and Siegfried Englemann, *Teaching Disadvantaged Children in the Preschool* (Englewood Cliffs, N.J.: Prentice-Hall, 1966).

38.   Committee of College and University Examiners, *Taxonomy of Educational Objectives: The Classification of Educational Goals*, ed. Benjamin Bloom (New York: David McKay, 1969).

39.   Arthur Whimbey and Linda Shaw Whimbey, *Intelligence Can Be Taught* (New York: Bantam Books, 1975), 89–93.

40.   Marvin Grosswirth and Abbie Salny, *The Mensa Genius Quiz Book* (New York: Addison-Wesley, 1981), 109.

41.   Stephen J. Morreale et al., "Temperature-Dependent Sex Determination: Current Practices Threaten Conservation of Sea Turtles," *Science* 216 (June 11, 1982): 1245–47.

After I discussed this concept with my young son Stuart, he produced a report of a similar study of temperature/sex determination in alligators: Rebecca Herman, "Contact Report," "3-2-1 Contact," *Children's Television Workshop*, April 1983. 23. (You never know where you'll find news.)

42.   Thomas G. Banville, *How to Listen—How to Be Heard* (Chicago: Nelson-Hall, 1978), 171–77.

43.   Leslie Kelly, Linda Comerford, Linda Perigo Moore, "Communication Flow Chart," in *Effective Business Writing*, 2nd ed. (Indianapolis: Kelly & Associates, 1983), II–1.

4: Please, God, If I Could Just Think of Something Really New

1. J. P. Guilford, "Creativity," *American Psychologist* 5 (1950): 444–54; J. P. Guilford, "Three Faces of Intellect, *American Psychologist* 14:8 (1959): 469–79.

2. J. W. Getzels and J. T. Dillon, "The Nature of Giftedness and the Education of the Gifted," in *The Gifted and The Talented*, ed. Roger Taylor (Englewood, Colo.: Educational Consulting Associates, 1975), 107–08.

3. Sharon Begley et al., "How the Brain Works," *Newsweek*, February 7, 1983, 40–47.

4. Ibid., 47.

5. Dean K. Simonton, "The Eminent Genius in History: The Critical Role of Creative Development," *Gifted Child Quarterly* 22:2 (Summer 1978): 187–95.

6. Getzels and Dillon, "The Nature of Giftedness," 107–08; R. Taft and M. B. Gilchrist, "Creative Attitudes and Creative Productivity: A Comparison of Two Aspects of Creativity Among Students," *Journal of Educational Psychology* 61 (1970): 136–43; Doreen A. Rosenthal and Maurice Conway, "Adolescents' Creativity and Non-Conformity in School," *Psychological Reports* 47:2 (October 1980): 668.

7. George Domino, "Creativity and the Home Environment," *Gifted Child Quarterly* 23:4 (Winter 1979): 818–28.

8. W. D. Buel, "Biographical Data and the Identification of Creative Research Personnel," *Journal of Applied Psychology* 49 (1965): 318–21.

9. John C. Dacey and George F. Madaus, "An Analysis of Two Hypotheses Concerning the Relationship Between Creativity and Intelligence," *The Journal of Educational Research* 64:5 (January 1971): 213–16; V. Goertzel and M. G. Goertzel, *Cradles of Eminence* (Boston: Little, Brown, 1962); M. G. Goertzel, V. Goertzel, and T. G. Goertzel, *300 Eminent Personalities* (San Francisco: Jossey-Bass, 1978); Gail A. Janquish and Richard Ripple, "Cognitive Creative Abilities and Self-Esteem Across the Adult Life Span," *Human Development* 24:2 (1981): 110–19.

10.   "Talent: Necessary But Not Sufficient," *Gifted Children Newsletter* 2:10 (October 1981): 3.

11.   Calvin W. Taylor and Diane Sacks, "Facilitating Lifetime Creative Processes—A Think Piece," *Gifted Child Quarterly* 25:3 (Summer 1981): 117.

12.   W. J. Smith et al., "The Prediction of Research Competence and Creativity from Personal History," *Journal of Applied Psychology* 45 (1961): 281–84.

13.   Calvin W. Taylor and R. L. Ellison, "Biographical Predictors of Scientific Performance," *Science* 155 (March 3, 1967): 1075–80.

14.   Bruce G. Whiting, "How to Predict Creativity from Biographical Data," *Journal of Creative Behavior* 7:3 (1973): 201–07.

15.   Frank Barron, *Creative Person and Creative Process* (New York: Holt, Rinehart and Winston, 1969).

16.   Harold K. Hughes, "The Enhancement of Creativity," *Journal of Creative Behavior* 3:2 (1969): 73–83; Thomas U. Busse and Richard S. Mansfield, "The Blooming of Creative Scientists: Early, Late and Otherwise," *Gifted Child Quarterly* 25:2 (Spring 1981): 63–66.

17.   H. R. Wallace, "Creative Thinking: A Factor in Sales Productivity," *Vocational Guidance Quarterly* 9 (1961): 223–26.

18.   Graham Wallas, *The Art of Thought* (London: C. A. Watts, 1926).

19.   Carl R. Rogers, "Toward a Theory of Creativity," in *A Sourcebook for Creative Thinking*, ed. S. J. Parnes and H. F. Harding (New York: Scribner's, 1962).

20.   B. D. Zimmerman and F. Dialessi, "Modeling Influences on Children's Creative Behavior," *Journal of Educational Psychology* 65 (1973): 127–35; T. L. Belcher, "Modeling Original Divergent Responses," *Journal of Applied Psychology* 67 (1975): 351–58.

21.   D. R. Ridley and R. C. Birney, "Effects of Training Procedures on Creativity Test Scores, *Journal of Educational Psychology* 58 (1967): 158–64.

22.   J. Holman, E. M. Goetz, and D. M. Baer, "The Train-

ing of Creativity as an Operant and an Examination of Its Generalization Characteristics," in *New Developments in Behavioral Research: Theory, Method and Application.* ed. B. C. Etzel and J. M. LeBlanc (Hillsdale, N.J.: Lawrence Erlbaum Associates, 1976).

23. Guilford, "Three Faces of Intellect," 444–54.

24. J. P. Guilford. *Way Beyond the IQ* (Buffalo, N.Y.: Creative Education Foundation, 1977).

25. J. P. Guilford, "Creativity: Its Measurement and Development," in *Assessing Creative Growth: The Tests—Book One*, ed. Angelo M. Biondi and Sidney J. Parnes (New York: Creative Synergetic Associates, 1976).

26. E. Paul Torrance. "Giftedness in Solving Future Problems," *Journal of Creative Behavior* 12:2 (Spring 1978): 75–86.

27. Frank Barron and David M. Harrington, "Creativity, Intelligence and Personality," *Annual Review of Psychology*, vol. 32, ed. Mark R. Rosenzweig and Lyman W. Porter (Palo Alto, Calif.: Annual Reviews, 1981), 440.

28. Joe Khatena, *The Creatively Gifted Child* (New York: Vantage Press, 1978), 51.

29. Barron and Harrington, "Creativity, Intelligence and Personality," 439–76.

30. E. Paul Torrance, "Examples and Rationales of Test Tasks for Assessing Creative Abilities," in Biondi and Parnes, *Assessing Creative Growth: The Tests—Book One.*

31. Sarnoff A. Mednick and Sharon Halpern, "The Remote Associates Test," in ibid.

32. John C. Flanagan, "Ingenuity Tests," in ibid.

33. E. Paul Torrance, *Torrance Tests of Creative Thinking, Manual* (Princeton, N.J.: Personnel Press, 1966).

34. J. P. Guilford, *Intelligence, Creativity and Their Educational Implications* (San Diego: Robert R. Knapp, 1968).

35. I. Maltzman, W. Bogartz, and L. A. Breger, "A Procedure for Increasing Word Association Originality and Its Transfer Effects," *Journal of Experimental Psychology* 56 (1958): 392–98.

36. J. L. Freeman, "Increasing Creativity by Free-

Association Training," *Journal of Experimental Psychology* 69 (1965): 89–91.

37.   Alex F. Osborn, *Applied Imagination: Principles and Procedures of Creative Thinking* (New York: Scribner's, 1953).

38.   Sidney J. Parnes and A. Meadow, "Effects of 'Brain-storming' Instructions on Creative Problem Solving by Trained and Untrained Subjects," *Journal of Educational Psychology* 50 (1959): 171–76.

39.   Sidney J. Parnes, "Effects of Extended Effort in Problem Solving," *Journal of Educational Psychology* 52 (1961): 117–22; S. J. Parnes and A. Meadow, "Evaluation of Persistence of Effects Produced by a Creative Problem Solving Course," *Psychological Reports* 7 (1960): 357–61.

40.   J. E. Arnold, "Useful Creative Techniques," in Parnes and Harding, *Sourcebook for Creative Thinking*.

41.   W. J. J. Gordon, *Synectics* (London: Collier Books, 1960).

42.   D. Miechenbaum, "Enhancing Creativity by Modifying What Subjects Say to Themselves," *American Educational Research Journal* 2 (1975):129–45.

5: The Smart Test
1.   Martin Gardner, *Mathematical Carnival* (New York: Alfred A. Knopf, 1975).

2.   Donovan Johnson et al., *Topology: The Rubber-Sheet Geometry* (St. Louis, Mo.: Webster Publishing Co., 1960).

3.   Willard R. Espy, *O Thou Improper, Thou Uncommon Noun* (New York: Clarkson N. Potter, 1978), 167.

Index

Ability
and creativity, 167
Ability grouping, 222n5
Ability to organize information,
226n13
Absorption, 167–68
Abstract reasoning, 17, 21, 41,
226n13
creativity and, 109
influenced by learning, 108
in IQ tests, 29
Academic display
genius as, 14
Accelerated learners, learning,
222–25n5
giftedness of, 14–16
thinking process of, 16–27
see also Gifted education
Achievement tests, 113
Acronyms, 175
as mnemonic association, 126–
27, 130
Action (decision making), 142
Adolescence, 225n9
Adrenaline, 226n13
Adult intelligence, 11–12, 107–61
IQ as definition of, 28
thinking skill areas in, 143–44
Adult learning, 11–12, 136

Advice giving (response style),
158
Affective skills, 108–09
Aging, 4
and learning, 9–12, 116
Albert Einstein College of Medicine, 37
Allen, Woody, 88
Alternate uses (exercise), 173
Alzheimer's disease, 9
Ambiguity, tolerance for, 167–68
*American Journal of Psycho-
analysis*, 8
American Psychologist (journal), 36
Ampère, André-Marie, 122
Analogical abilities (creative
process), 175–76
Analogy(ies)
false, 87
solving of, 54–55
see also Figural analogies;
Verbal analogies
Analysis (thinking skill), 106,
108, 133, 134–35, 136, 137,
161, 163
of components, 144
defined, 76
increasing skills of, 144–50